Outrageous

After-Dinner
Jokes & Stories

PPGS
LONDON

First published in Great Britain by
PPGS
PO Box 42
Princes Risborough
Bucks.
HP27 0XH

© PPGS/KCS 2001

ISBN 0-9540822-0-6

Production by Omnipress, Eastbourne

Printed in Denmark

Confucious he say ....

"Man who take girl in park,
have peace on earth"

Bu-Wangy!

Ron, a tall, handsome and successful businessman, was in Tokyo for the first time, and whilst in a Bar, pulled a local girl. They got on very well, despite neither being able to speak the other's language.

One thing led to the other and the international sign language of love took its usual course and they ended up in Ron's room. They were getting down to it well, with the Japanese girl constantly moving round, trying all different positions. Ron was utterly amazed and confused by the contortions she was performing in the dark. All he knew was that she was wonderfully tight and at one point he had to really hang on as she rode him hard. She was yelling, Bu-Wangy, Bu-Wangy! Bu-Wangy, Bu-Wangy! Not understanding the language, but feeling close to exploding in this woman, he knew she must be feeling this, so he thrust faster and faster until they collapsed together in a heap on the bed. What a great night!

 Next Day on a local golf course with his new found Japanese business colleagues, Ron was keen to show he had acquired some local knowledge. His mind was thinking back to the night before, and thought, now what did she say when I really gave her a portion, ah yes, Bu-Wangy – I was so good, that it must mean fabulous or brilliant. So when a couple of holes later, one of the Japanese sunk a 40 foot putt, Ron burst into action. I'll impress them he thought. He clapped and yelled Bu-Wangy, Bu-Wangy! Some very strange looks came his way, but Ron thought, wow, they must be so impressed with my knowledge of their language, that really took them aback.

The very next hole, one of the other Japanese golfers chipped in from 45 yards. Again Ron, now feeling great about himself, yelled out, Bu-Wangy, Bu-Wangy! Ron's main business contact walked slowly and deliberately across the green towards Ron, and said "They told me you velly expelienced golfer Lon, so why you keep shout, Wrong Hole, Wrong Hole?"

NO SEX IN CHURCH

Three couples, an elderly couple, a middle-aged couple and a young newlywed couple wanted to join a church.

The Reverend said, "We have special requirements for new parishioners. You must abstain from having sex for two weeks."

The couples agreed and came back at the end of two weeks.

The Reverend went to the elderly couple and asked, "Were you able to abstain from sex for the two weeks?"
The old man replied, "No problem at all, Reverend."

"Congratulations! Welcome to the church", said the Reverend.

The Reverend went to the middle-aged couple and asked, "Well, were you able to abstain from sex for the two weeks?"
The man replied, "The first week was not too bad. The second week I had to sleep on the couch for a couple of nights but, yes, we made it."

"Congratulations! Welcome to the church", said the Reverend.

The Reverend then went to the newlywed couple and asked, "Well, were you able to abstain from sex for two weeks?"
 "No, Reverend, we were not able to go without sex for the two weeks," the young man replied sadly. "My wife was reaching for a can of paint on the top shelf and dropped it. When she bent over to pick it up, I was overcome with lust and took advantage of her right there."

The Reverend said, sympathetically, "You understand, of course, this means you will not be welcome in our church".

"We know" said the young man,

"We're not welcome at B&Q any more, either!"

CUTTING THE ICE

A drunk decides to go ice fishing, so he gathers his gear and goes walking around until he finds a big patch of ice.
He heads into the centre of the ice and begins to saw a hole.

All of a sudden, a loud booming voice comes out of the sky.
"You will find no fish under that ice."

The drunk looks around, but sees no one.
He starts sawing again.
Once more, the voice speaks,
"As I said before, there are no fish under the ice."

The drunk looks all around, high and low, but can't see a single soul.
He picks up the saw and tries one more time to finish. Before he can even start cutting, the huge voice interrupts.
"I have warned you three times now.
There are **no** fish!"

The drunk is now flustered and somewhat scared, so he asks the voice,
"How do you know there are no fish? Are you God trying to warn me?"

"No", the voice replied.

"Who are you then?", asked the drunk, now really scared.

"I am the Manager of this ice rink."

Carlos The Ice Cream Man

Carlos the ice-cream man's van is parked at the side of the road. Lights flashing, music playing, a big queue of excited kids stretches down the street.

But no sign of Carlos.

A policeman walking down the road wonders what is going on. Where is Carlos?

Why is he not dishing out the ice cream?

He went over to the van and peered over the high counter. On the floor he spotted Carlos.

Lying very still covered in chocolate sauce, strawberry sauce, nuts, hundreds and thousands and those little jelly bits.

"Get back kids," he shouts.

Moving away so the bemused kids cannot overhear him he gets on the radio to the station.

"Sarge, get someone down here quick," he stutters, "It's Carlos the ice-cream man...

He's topped himself."

A Ciggie Brolly

Two old ladies were waiting for a bus and one of them was smoking a cigarette. It started to rain, so the old lady reached into her purse, took out a condom, cut off the tip and slipped it over her cigarette and continued to smoke.

Her friend saw this and said, "Hey that's a good idea! What is it that you put over your cigarette?"

The other old lady said, "It's a condom."

"A condom? Where do you get those?"

The lady with the cigarette told her friend that you could purchase condoms at the chemist.

When the two old ladies arrived downtown, the old lady with all the questions went into the chemist and asked the pharmacist if he sold condoms. The pharmacist said yes, but looked a little surprised that this old woman was interested in condoms, so he asked her, "What size do you want?"

The old lady thought for a minute and said,
"One that will fit a Camel!"

~~~~~~~~

INDECISION

is the key to

FLEXIBILITY.

SPOT!

A young man was delighted to finally be asked home to meet the parents of the young woman he'd been seeing for some time.

He was quite nervous about the meeting, though, and by the time he arrived punctually at the doorstep he was in a state of gastric distress.

The problem developed into one of acute flatulence, and halfway through the dinner the young man realised he couldn't hold it in one second longer without exploding.

A tiny fart escaped.

"SPOT!" called out the young woman's mother to the family dog, lying at the young man's feet. Relieved at the dog having been blamed, the young man relaxed a little and let another, slightly larger one go.

"Spot!" she called out sharply.

"I've got it made," thought the fellow to himself. One more and I'll feel fine. So he let loose a really big one.

"Spot!" shrieked the mother. "Get over here before he shits on you!"

<u>WANTED</u>

A tall well-built woman with good

reputation, who can cook frogs

legs, who appreciates a good fuc-

schia garden, classic music and tal-

king without getting too serious.

Now read it again, but this time only read lines 1, 3 and 5.

1-2-3 JUMP!

In a National Hunt Race at Aintree, a jockey takes a tumble and breaks his collarbone in the race before a really important race. The trainer hurriedly employs the services of an old pro who is a little past his sell-by date. In briefing the old pro on the horse, the trainer insists to the jockey that with this horse you have to assist him over the jumps by yelling 1-2-3 jump! as he approaches each fence. If he does that, the horse has a great chance of romping away with this race.

The old pro jockey mounts the horse and canters down to the start, thinking to himself that they must think he is wet behind the ears. Can you imagine his credibility with the other jockeys, if they heard him going 1-2-3 jump! Before each fence! They'd think he really had lost it!

The race begins and the horse instantly builds up a lead of 2 lengths before the first jump. As they come into it, the jockey decides not to do this silly 1-2-3 bit and the horse just bulldozes straight through the fence, nearly unseating the rider in the process. The next 2 fences the horse, despite a tug on the bridle to lift his head up over the jumps, just bulldozes straight through the fence. There are bits of twig and leaves now hanging off both horse and jockey and most of the field have past him by. Other jockeys are shouting, "It's the jump season now dickhead!" as they stride by. He is feeling as if he's got a real bum ride here as the horse crashes through yet another fence. Now 4 lengths adrift at the back with only 5 fences to go, he decides to try this stupid 1-2-3 jump! And lo and behold, the horse sails over the fence so smoothly that he can visibly see the horse in front closer already.

The jockey thinks "Well bugger me, if this works I may save a bit of my reputation in the weighing room afterwards" Next jump, 1-2-3- jump! And the horse sails over again. Only 3 to go now and he's past the 2 back markers. Next jump 1-2-3- jump!, In the middle of the pack now, and after the next jump, he's lying 3rd and going like a train. The other jockeys are shouting at him, but he's ignoring them now. The last jump; 1-2-3 jump! Straight over and neck and neck with the leader. It's a 2-furlong run to the line and his horse is flying. Over the line nearly 2 lengths ahead and he's feeling pretty pleased with himself despite bits of twig still stuck under the saddle.

The owner and trainer meet him in the unsaddling enclosure.

"What the hell did you think you were doing" the trainer yells at him. "That was the most dreadful exhibition of jockeyship I've ever seen. You didn't talk him over the fences at the beginning."
"The horse couldn't hear me" he lied.
"The horse is not deaf, it's blind!" said the trainer.

8

CUSTOMER SERVICE

<u>For all of you out there who've had to deal with an irate customer,
this one is for you.</u>

In tribute to those 'special' customers we all love! An award
should go to the United Airlines gate agent in Denver for being
smart and funny, and making her point, when confronted with a
passenger who probably deserved to fly as cargo.

A crowded United Airlines flight was cancelled.

A single agent was rebooking a long line of inconvenienced
travellers.
Suddenly an angry passenger pushed his way to the desk, he
slapped his ticket down on the counter and said,
"I **HAVE** to be on this flight and it **HAS** to be **FIRST CLASS**."
The agent replied,
"I'm sorry sir, I'll be happy to try to help you, but I've got to help
these folks first, and I'm sure we'll be able to work something
out."

The passenger was unimpressed. He asked loudly, so that the
passengers behind him could hear,
"Do you have any idea who I am?"

Without hesitating, the gate agent smiled and grabbed her public
address microphone, "May I have your attention please?" she
began, her voice bellowing throughout the terminal.
"We have a passenger here at the gate **WHO DOES NOT KNOW
WHO HE IS**. If anyone can help him find his identity, please
come to the gate."

With the folks behind him in line laughing hysterically, the man
glared at the United agent, gritted his teeth and swore,
"F*** you!"

Without flinching, she smiled and said,

"I'm sorry, sir, but you'll have to stand in line for that, too."

The Computer – Male or Female?

A language instructor was explaining to her class that French nouns, unlike their English counterparts, are grammatically designated as masculine or feminine. Things like "chalk" or "pencil," she described, would have a gender association. For example: House is feminine – "la" maison. In English, of course, words are of neutral gender.

Puzzled, one student raised his hand and asked,
"What gender is a computer?"

The teacher wasn't certain which it was, and so divided the class into two groups and asked them to decide if a computer should be masculine or feminine. One group was composed of the women in the class, and the other of men. Both groups were asked to give four reasons for their recommendation.

The men decided that computers should definitely be referred to in the <u>feminine gender (la)</u> because:

1. No one but their creator understands their internal logic.
2. The native language they use to communicate with other computers is incomprehensible to everyone else.
3. Even the smallest mistakes are stored in long-term memory for later retrieval.
4. As soon as you make a commitment to one, you find yourself spending half your salary on accessories for it.

The group of women, however, concluded that computers should be referred to in the <u>masculine (le) gender</u> because:
1. In order to get their attention, you have to turn them on.
2. They have a lot of data but are still clueless.
3. They are supposed to help you solve your problems, but half the time they ARE the problem.
4. As soon as you commit to one, you realise that, if you had waited a little longer, you could have had a better model.

007 – Licensed to Thrill

James Bond walks into a bar and takes a seat next to an
astoundingly beautiful woman.
He shoots her a look.

The woman notices him glance at his watch so asks,
"Your date running late?"
"No," he replies,
"I've been given a state-of-the-art watch by Q.
Thought I'd test it out."

She takes hold of his wrist to have a closer look.
"It's nice, but 'state-of-the-art'? What's so special about it?"

"Well, it uses alpha waves to uncover secrets held by those
around me."
"What's it telling you now?" she said.

Bond looks round and whispers,
"It says you're not wearing any knickers."

Laughing she replies, "I'm afraid your watch must be
broken."

Bond tuts and tweaks the dial. "Must be an hour fast."

MY Life – Oivay!

Abie: "Sara, I have tried to be a good husband but I have to tell you that unless I can find five thousand pounds by tomorrow, I will go bankrupt."

Sara: "Abie, in the drawer beside the bed you will find six thousand pounds. I have saved this by putting ten pounds in there every time you have made love to me."

Abie: "Sara, what a brilliant girl you are. If only you had told me this before, I would have given you all of my business!"

~~~~~~~~~~~~~~~~~~~~

Jewish dilemma: A half-price offer on a bacon sandwich!

~~~~~~~~~~~~~~~~~~~~

Life's A Lottery!

Abie went into the synagogue and prayed.
"God, you've got to help me win the lottery, I'm desperate,
I owe money to everyone."
Next week he was back again.
"God," he said "If I don't win the lottery this week I'm
a ruined man."
Suddenly a big voice boomed from the sky:
"Abie! Please! Meet me Half Way.
Buy a Ticket!"

~~~~~~~~~~~~~~~~~~~

Jewish Foreplay: Two hours of begging and pleading!

~~~~~~~~~~~~~~~~~~~

Why do Jewish men die before their wives?
Because they want to!

~~~~~~~~~~~~~~~~~~~

THE TWO FRENCH PARATROOPERS

Two French paratroopers were seconded to the SAS for some special training. After the first day, they met up in the bar.

"Ah Pierre" says one. "What 'av you been doing?"

"Oh" says Pierre, "I 'av 'ad a terrible day. Terrible! At seex o'clock zis morning I was woken by zis big 'airy SAS sergeant. He dragged me out of bed and out onto ze parade ground."

"What 'appened next?" asks his mate.

"I will tell you what 'appened! He made me climb up zis silly leetle platform five feet off ze ground and he said 'jump'."

After Dinner CLASSIC!

"Oh" says his mate. "And did you jump?"

"I did not" says Pierre. "I told 'im – I am a French Paratrooper. I do not jump five feet. It is below my dignity."

"And what 'appened then?" asks his mate.

"Then he made me climb up a silly leetle platform ten feet off ze ground and 'e said 'jump'."

"Did you jump?" asks the mate.

"I did not jump. I told 'im – I am a French Paratrooper. It is below my dignity to jump ten feet."

"And what 'appened next?" says his mate.

"Zen he made me climb up zis rickety platform a 'undred feet above ze parade ground. 'e undid 'is trousers, took out zis enormous willy and 'e said 'If you do not jump, I am going to stick zis right up your burm'.

"Ooooh" says his mate. "And did you jump?"

"A leetle, at first".

14

Ladies (?) On The Golf Course

A foursome is waiting at the men's tee while another foursome of ladies are hitting from the ladies tee.

The ladies are taking their time and when finally the last one is ready to hit the ball she hacks it about 10 feet, goes over to it and hacks it another 10 feet, looks up at the men, who are watching, and says apologetically:

"I guess all those fucking lessons I took this winter didn't help."

One of the men immediately replies, "No, you see that's your problem. You should have taken 'golf lessons' instead."

~~~~~~~~~~~~~~~~~~

What IS a Lesbian?

Yet another Woman trying to do a Man's Job!

~~~~~~~~~~~~~~~~~~

<u>BLOW THAT!</u>

A young woman walks up and sits down at the bar.
"What can I get you?" the bartender inquires.

"I want 6 shots of Jack Daniels" responded the young woman.
"6 shots?!? Are you celebrating something?"
"Yeah, my first blowjob."
"Well, in that case, let me give you a 7th on the house."

"No offence, sir.
But if 6 shots won't get rid of the taste, nothing will."

~~~~~~~~~~~~~~~~~~~~~

Did you hear about the Irish Lesbian?

She's into fellers!

If you can stay calm, while all around you there is chaos... then you probably haven't completely understood the seriousness of the situation.

Hello Big Boy!

A businessman boards a flight and is lucky enough to be seated next to an absolutely gorgeous woman.

They exchange brief hellos and he notices she is reading a manual about sexual statistics.

He asks her about it and she replies,

"This is a very interesting book about sexual statistics. It identifies that American Indians have the longest average penis and Polish men have the biggest average diameter.

By the way, my name is Jill. What's yours?"

He drawled, coolly,
"Tonto Jablonski, nice to meet you."

~~~~~~~~~~~~~~~~~~~

Doctor, Doctor, help me.
I keep thinking I'm a bridge.
What's come over you?
3 buses, 6 cars and an articulated truck!

Are You Going To Sleep, or What?

One night, as a couple lay down for bed, the husband gently taps his wife on the shoulder and starts rubbing her arm. The wife turns over and says,

"I'm sorry darling, I've got a gynaecologist appointment tomorrow and I want to stay fresh."

The husband, rejected, turns over and tries to sleep.

A few minutes later, he rolls back over and taps his wife again. This time he whispers in her ear,

"Do you have a dentist appointment tomorrow too?"

~~~~~~~~~~~~~~~~~~~~~

If you choke a smurf, what colour does it turn?

What A Choker!

A man is visiting his wife in hospital where she has been in a coma for several years. On this visit he decides to rub her left breast instead of just talking to her. On doing this she lets out a sigh. The man runs out and tells the doctor who says this is a good sign and suggests he should try rubbing her right breast to see if there is any reaction.

The man goes in and rubs her right breast and this brings a moan from his wife. He rushes out and tells the doctor.

The doctor says this is amazing and is a real break through. The doctor then suggests the man should go in and try oral sex, saying he will wait outside as it is a personal act and he doesn't want the man to be embarrassed.

The man goes in then comes out about five minutes later, white as a sheet and tells the doctor his wife is dead.

The doctor asks what happened to which the man replies,

"She choked."

Turner Brown

A small white guy goes into an elevator, when he gets in he notices a huge black dude standing next to him. The big black dude looks down upon the small white guy and says,
"7 foot tall, 350 pounds, 20 inch dick, 3 pound left ball, 3 pound right ball, Turner Brown."

The small white guy faints !!

The big black dude picks up the small white guy and brings him to, slapping his face and shaking him and asks the small white guy

"What's wrong?"

The small white guy says,
"Excuse me but what did you say?" The big black dude looks down and says "7 foot tall, 350 pounds, 20 inch dick, 3 pound left ball, 3 pound right ball, my name is Turner Brown."

The small white guy let out a huge sigh of relief and said

"Thank god, I thought you said "Turn around."

The Singing Golfer

A man went to the doctor with a strange complaint.

"Well it's like this Doc, whenever I play golf, I fall in love with the beautiful, lush fairways and greens we are playing on, and I just burst into song."
"What's wrong with that?" said the doc.
Well all I ever sing when we're on the course is 'The Green Green Grass of Home' and it's pissing off my colleagues.

But there's more….When we get back to the clubhouse, in the bar is the lucky black cat that lives at the club, then at the top of my voice I start singing" 'What's new, pussy cat?' and all I get is a barrage of complaint from the other members in the bar.

"Can't you sing some different tunes?" said the doctor.
"Well no, I just can't seem to sing anything else, but then it gets worse because when I get home, it continues and when I'm asleep and dreaming, I always sing 'Delilah', and my wife is increasingly getting really angry and suspicious.
But I just can't seem to stop singing these same tunes"

"Ah, yes I see, I am beginning to suspect that you have the early symptoms of Tom Jones syndrome".

"Well I've never heard of that, is it common?" asked the man.

"It's not unusual", replied the doctor.

Strange Things Happen On
A Golf Course

A man goes to the confessional.
"Forgive me father, for I have sinned."
"What is your sin, my son?" the priest asks back.
"Well," the man starts, "I used some awful language this week and feel absolutely terrible."

When did you use this awful language?" asks the priest.
"Well, I was golfing and hit an incredible drive that looked like it was going to go over 280 yards, but it struck a phone line that was hanging over the fairway and fell straight down to the ground after going only about 100 yards."

"Is that when you swore?"
No, Father," says the man.
"After that, a squirrel ran out of the bushes and grabbed my ball in his mouth and began to run away."

"Is THAT when you swore?" asks the Father again.
"Well, no." says the man. "You see, as the squirrel was running, an eagle came down out of the sky, grabbed the squirrel in his talons and began to fly away!"

"Is THAT when you swore?" asks the amazed Priest.
"No, not yet," the man replies. "As the eagle carried the squirrel away in his claws, it flew over a bit of forest near the green and the squirrel dropped my ball."

"Did you swear THEN?" asked the impatient Priest.
"No, because as the ball fell, it struck a tree, bounced through some bushes, careered off a big rock, and rolled through a sand trap onto the green and stopped within six inches of the hole."

Silence filled the confessional until the Priest sighed and said,

"Don't tell me you missed the fucking putt?"

The Ambidextrous Golfer

A golf league was looking to replace a member who had left the league. They saw a fellow on the course who looked very promising and invited him to join them the next Saturday.

"Okay," the fellow said, "at the same time? Fine, I'll be there. I might be 15 minutes late, but I'll be there."
Sure enough, the next week he showed up promptly at 8am.
He shot a beautiful game left-handed. The rest of the fellows were pleased with him and his game, and they asked him to return the following week for another round of golf.

"Sure," said the golfer. "I'll be here same time, same place. I might be 15 minutes late, but I'll be here."

The next week he showed up right on time and had another great game which he played right-handed.
The other fellows noted his ambidexterity, and one of them said, "What's with you? One week you play left handed, the next week you play right handed! How come?"

"It depends on my wife," said the new league member.
"When I wake up, if she's sleeping on her left side, I go out and play golf left-handed. And if she's sleeping on her right side, I play a right handed game."
"But what if she's sleeping on her back? Asked the questioner.

"Then I'm 15 minutes late!" was the reply.

A Lion Bar

A guy walks into a bar with a pet lion by his side. He puts the lion up on the bar. He turns to the astonished patrons.

"I'll make you a deal. I'll open this lion's mouth and place my genitals inside. Then the lion will close his mouth for one minute. He'll then open his mouth and I'll remove my unit unscathed.

In return for witnessing this spectacle, each of you will buy me a drink."

The crowd murmured their approval. The man stood up on the bar, dropped his trousers, and placed his privates in the lion's open mouth. The lion closed his mouth as the crowd gasped. After a minute, the man grabbed a beer bottle and rapped the lion hard on the top of its head. The lion opened his mouth and the man removed his genitals – unscathed as promised.

The crowd cheered and the first of his free drinks was delivered.

The man stood up again and made another offer.
"I'll pay anyone $100 who's willing to give it a try".
A hush fell over the crowd.

After a while, a hand went up in the back of the bar.
A woman timidly spoke up.

"I'll try, but you have to promise not to hit me on the head with the beer bottle."

What A Pickle!

Bill worked in a pickle factory. He had been employed there for a number of years when he came home one day to confess to his wife that he had a terrible compulsion. He had an urge to stick his penis into the pickle slicer.

His wife suggested that he should see a sex therapist to talk about it, but Bill indicated that he'd be too embarrassed. He vowed to overcome the compulsion on his own.

One day a few weeks later, Bill came home absolutely ashen. His wife could see at once that something was seriously wrong. "What's wrong, Bill?" she asked.

"Do you remember that I told you how I had this tremendous urge to put my penis into the pickle slicer?"

"Oh, Bill, you didn't."
"Yes, I did."
"My God, Bill, what happened?"
"I got fired."

"No, Bill. I mean, what happened with the pickle slicer?"
"Oh...she got fired too."

What A Load Of Bull!

A man takes his wife to the County Show.
They start heading down the alley that houses all the bulls.
The sign on the first bull's stall states:
"This bull mated 50 times last year."

The wife turns to her husband and says,
"He mated 50 times in a year, isn't that nice!"

They proceed to the next bull and his sign stated:
"This bull mated 65 times last year."
The wife turns to her husband and says, "This one mated 65
times last year. That is over 5 times a month. You could learn
from this one!"

They proceeded to the last bull and his sign said:
"This bull mated 365 times last year."
The wife's mouth drops open and says, "WOW! He mated 365
times last year. That is ONCE A DAY!!
You could really learn from this one."

The fed up man turns to his wife and says,
"Go up and ask if it was 365 times with the
same cow."

~~~~~~~~~~~~~~~~~~~~

The angry wife met her husband at the door. There was alcohol on
his breath and lipstick on his collar. "I assume," she snarled, "that
there is a very good reason for you to come waltzing in here at six
o'clock in the morning?"
"There is," he replied. "Breakfast."

Women's Revenge

SOME for the girls...

Why do men become smarter during sex?
Because they are plugged into a genius.

Why don't women blink during foreplay?
They don't have time.

Why don't women have men's brains?
Because they don't have penises to put them in.

What do electric trains and breasts have in common?
They're intended for children, but it's the men who usually end up playing with them.

Why do men snore when they lay on their backs?
Because their balls fall over their assholes and they vapour lock.

Why do men masturbate?
It's sex with someone they love.

Why were men given larger brains than dogs?
So they won't hump women's legs at cocktail parties.

How many honest, intelligent, caring men in the world does it take to do the dishes?
Both of them.

Why does it take one million sperm to fertilize one egg?
They won't stop to ask directions.

What do men and sperm have in common?
They both have a one-in-a-million chance of becoming a human being.

Golf Balls!

A guy out on the golf course takes a high-speed ball right in the crotch. Writhing in agony, he falls to the ground. As soon as he could manage, he took himself to the doctor.
He said, "How bad is it doc? I'm going on my honeymoon next week and my fiancée is still a virgin in every way."

The doctor told him, "I'll have to put your penis in a splint to let it heal and keep it straight. It should be okay next week."
So he took four tongue depressors and formed a neat little 4-sided bandage, and wired it all together; an impressive work of art.

The guy mentions none of this to his girl, marries and goes on their honeymoon. That night in their honeymoon suite, she rips open her blouse to reveal a gorgeous set of breasts. This was the first time he had seen them.
She said, "You're the first, no one has ever touched these breasts."

Thinking quickly about how not to disappoint her at this vital time, he drops his pants and says,
"Look at this, mine's still in it's CRATE!"

~~~~~~~~~~~~~~~~~~~~~~

Quickies!

Bob met this utterly fantastic Blonde with a stuck-up attitude.

She said "I don't go to bed with any guy unless he's got a 12 inch cock."

Bob said "Oh Bollocks then, I'm not cutting off 2 inches for anyone!"

~~~~~~~~~~~~~~~~~~~~

Two blondes walking down the street. One notices a compact on the path and picks it up. She opens it, looks in the mirror and says "hey, this person looks familiar". "Here, let me see" says the second blonde. She looks in the mirror and says "of course it does, you dickhead, its me!"

~~~~~~~~~~~~~~~~~~~~

Little Johnny was caught by his mother having a wank in the bath.
"You mustn't do that to your willy" she said.
"Why not, it's mine and I'll wash it as fast as I like!"

~~~~~~~~~~~~~~~~~~~~

• Why did God give women a vagina?

• So Men would talk to them!

German Efficiency

A German chap asks a prostitute for a shag and she tells him it's 50 dollars. "Fine" he says, "but I'm a bit kinky." She agrees that this is OK as long as he doesn't do anything violent.

They get back to her flat and he gets out four big springs attached to some straps.

"I want you to put one of these on each elbow and one on each knee" he asks. The prostitute is worried that she's getting into something a bit heavy, but she goes along with his request. Then she is told to get down on all fours, naked, in front of him, which she does grudgingly. Then he asks her to start bouncing up and down on the springs and finally he takes a duck call whistle from his pocket.

"Blow on this while I am shagging you" he tells her. So he's banging away at her from behind while she's bouncing on the springs blowing the duck whistle. Suddenly she starts to enjoy the shagging, so much so in fact that she experiences the most fantastic orgasm she's ever had.

After they've finished she says "Wow, that was the most fantastic sex I've had in 25 years on the game, how the hell did you make it so good?"

"Ah," he replies, "Foursprung Duck Technique".

Balls!

A little old lady went into the Bank of Canada one day, carrying a bag of money. She insisted that she must speak with the president of the bank to open a savings account because, "It's a lot of money!"

After much humming and hawing, the bank staff finally ushered her into the president's office (the customer is always right!).

The bank president then asked her how much she would like to deposit. She replied,"$165,000!" and dumped the cash out of her bag onto his desk.

The president was of course curious as to how she came by all this cash, so he asked her, "Ma'am, I'm surprised you're carrying so much cash around. Where did you get this money?"

The old lady replied, "I make bets."

The president then asked, "Bets? What kind of bets?"

The old woman said, "Well, for example, I'll bet you $25,000 that your balls are square."

"Ha!" laughed the president, "That's a stupid bet. You can never win that kind of bet!"

The old lady challenged, "So, would you like to take my bet?"

"Sure," said the president, "I'll bet $25,000 that my balls are not square!" The little old lady then said, "Okay, but since there is a lot of money involved, may I bring my lawyer with me tomorrow at 10:00 am as a witness?" "Sure!" replied the very confident president.

That night, the president got very nervous about the bet and spent a long time in front of a mirror checking his balls, turning from side to side, again and again. He thoroughly checked them out until he was sure that there was absolutely no way his balls were square and that he would win the bet.

The next morning, at precisely 10:00 am, the little old lady appeared with her lawyer at the president's office. She introduced the lawyer to the president and repeated the bet: "$25,000 says the president's balls are square!" The president agreed with the bet again and the old lady asked him to drop his pants so they could all see. The president complied.

The little old lady peered closely at his balls and then asked if she could feel them. "Well, Okay," said the president,"$25,000 is a lot of money, so I guess you should be absolutely sure."

Just then, he noticed that the lawyer was quietly banging his head against the wall. The president asked the old lady, "What the hell's the matter with your lawyer?"

She replied, "Nothing, except I bet him $100,000 that at 10:00 am today, I'd have the President of The Bank of Canada's balls in my hand."

Froggies!

This woman is walking by a pet shop and she sees a sign in the Window that says 'Fanny-licking Frogs'. So she reckons I'll have a bit of this, goes in and the guy in the shop says "you're in luck, this is our last one". So she pays her money and heads home and that night strips off, lies on the bed and puts the frog between her legs...but nothing happens.

After a while she gives up, and decides to try the following night. But the next night there are no results, and none the night after that.

So she decides to bring the frog back to the pet shop.

She storms in and says, "What's the fucking story with this frog?"

The guy in the shop says, "Right, I'll sort this fella out". So he brings her out back and gets her to undress.

He puts the frog on the table and says,

"Now this is the last time I'll show you how to do this..."

Food For Thought...

Why do they lock petrol station toilets?
Are they afraid someone will clean them?

What was the best thing before sliced bread?

Why is there only one monopolies commission?

What happens if you get scared half to death twice?

The Early bird gets the worm, but
the second mouse gets the cheese

Atheism is a non-prophet organisation

A "Little Johnny" Story

The new Teacher walked into the classroom one sunny spring morning.
"Good Morning Children!"
"I am your new teacher and I want you to learn and remember my name very carefully.
You will call me Miss Franny."

"Now to help you learn it, I will give a special prize of a very large bag of sweets to the first child who can correctly say my name tomorrow morning."

Little Johnny was really motivated by the thought of a huge bag of sweets, so all the way home he kept saying to himself, Miss Franny, Miss Franny, but after having got distracted by his friends he tried again. Miss….er   Fra……oh yes FRANNY!

I'll try a better way of remembering he thought. Lets try Fanny with an R, Fanny with an R, Fanny with an R, Fanny with an R, Fanny with an R, Fanny with an R. By the time he got home he thought he'd got that off okay and would surely win the sweets.

The following morning, Miss Franny came into the classroom and said cheerfully,
"Good Morning Children!"
Johnny, determined not to be beaten, and shaking with anticipation and excitement, could wait no longer and burst out at the top of his voice….
"Morning Miss Crunt" he yelled!

~~~~~~~~~~~~~~~~~~~~

Just Like That!

Time for your Tommy Cooper Voice.........

"So I was getting into my car, and this bloke says to me 'Can you give me a lift?' I said "Sure, you look great, the world's your oyster, go for it."

~~~~~~~~~~~~~~~~~~~

"You know, somebody actually complimented me on my driving today.
They left a little note on the windscreen; it said 'Parking Fine.'
So that was nice."

~~~~~~~~~~~~~~~~~~~

"So I went down my local ice-cream shop, and said
'I'd like to buy an ice-cream.'

He said 'Hundreds & thousands?' I said 'We'll start with one.'
He said 'Knickerbocker glory?'
I said 'I do get a certain amount of freedom in these trousers, yes.'"

~~~~~~~~~~~~~~~~~~~

"My old Dad told me, 1 in 5 people in the world are Chinese. And there are 5 people in my family, so it must be one of them.
It's either my mum or my dad.
Or my older brother Colin.
Or my younger brother Ho-Cha-Chu.

But I think it's Colin."

The Balance of Power – Down Under?

Once upon a time in the kingdom of Heaven, God went missing for six days. Eventually, Michael the Archangel found him. He inquired of God, "Where were you?"

God sighed a deep sigh of satisfaction and proudly pointed downwards through the clouds; "Look son, look what I've made". Archangel Michael looked puzzled and said, "What is it?" God replied, "It's a planet and I've put LIFE on it. I've named it Earth and there is a balance between everything on it.

For example, there's North America and South America. North America is going to be rich and South America is going to be poor, and the narrow bit joining them - that's going to be a hot spot.

Now look over here. I've put a continent of white people in the north and another one of black people in the south. That's Europe and Africa.

The Archangel then said, "And what's that long broken white line there?" And God said "Ah - that is New Zealand - the land of the long white cloud and that's a very special place."

"That's going to be the most glorious spot on earth;"

"Beautiful Mountains, lakes, rivers, streams, and an exquisite coast-line."

"The people there are going to be modest, intelligent and humorous and they're going to be found travelling the world. They'll be extremely sociable, hard working and high achieving. And I'm going to give them this superhuman, undefeatable rugby team which will be blessed with the most talented, and charismatic specimens on the planet, and will be admired and feared by all who come across them."

Michael the Archangel gasped in wonder and admiration but then seeming startled proclaimed: "Hold on a second, what about the BALANCE? You said there was going to be a balance."

God replied wisely.
"Wait until you see the irritating loud-mouthed wankers I'm putting in the country next to them.

37

After Quasimodo

After Quasimodo's death, the Bishop of the Cathedral of Notre Dame sent word through the streets of Paris that a new bellringer was needed. The Bishop decided that he would conduct the interviews personally and went up into the belfry to begin the screening process.

After observing several applicants demonstrate their skills, he decided to call it a day, when a lone, armless man approached him and announced that he was there to apply for the bellringers job. The Bishop was incredulous. "You have no arms!" "No matter," said the man, "observe!" He then began striking the bells with his face, producing a beautiful melody on the carillon. The Bishop listened in astonishment, convinced that he had finally found a suitable replacement for Quasimodo.

Suddenly, rushing forward to strike a bell, the armless man tripped, and plunged headlong out of the belfry window to his death in the street below. The stunned Bishop rushed to his side. When he reached the street, a crowd had gathered around the fallen figure, drawn by the beautiful music they had heard only moments before. As they silently parted to let the Bishop through, one of them asked, "Bishop, who was this man?"

"I don't know his name," the Bishop sadly replied, "but his face rings a bell."

{WAIT! There's more!}

The following day, despite the sadness that weighed heavily on his heart due to the unfortunate death of the armless campanologist, the Bishop continued his interviews for a new bellringer of Notre Dame. The first man to approach him said,

"Your excellency, I am the brother of the poor, armless wretch that fell to his death from this very belfry yesterday. I pray that you honour his life by allowing me to replace him in this duty."

The Bishop agreed to give the man an audition, and as the armless man's brother stooped to pick up a mallet to strike the first bell, he groaned, clutched at his chest and died on the spot. Two monks, hearing the Bishop's cries of grief at this second tragedy, rushed up the stairs to his side.

"What has happened?" the first breathlessly asked, "Who is this man?"

"I don't know his name," sighed the distraught bishop, "but he's a dead ringer for his brother."

PADDY WANTS TO BE A MILLIONAIRE!

PADDY is on half a million and Chris Tarrant says to him, Paddy, for £1 million I want you to look at this picture of a famous person as a baby and tell me who it is.
Your only clue is that he is now a very famous footballer.

Paddy looks at the picture and says "to be sure it's David Beckham."
Tarrant says "is that your final answer?"

Paddy thinks hard.

Chris Tarrant says "would you like to phone a friend?
"Ah yes" says Paddy, "I'll phone Murphy, he's always right about everything."

Paddy gets through to Murphy and says "Do you know who it is Murphy?"
Without hesitation Murphy says, "To be sure, to be sure, it's Ryan Giggs."

Paddy says to Chris Tarrant "It's Ryan Giggs."

Tarrant says "Is that your final answer?"

Paddy says "Yes sir, it sure is."

Chris Tarrant says very slowly,
"Paddy, I'm really gutted to have to tell you that you've just lost £1million."

"The correct answer is Andy Cole."

Did You Know?

• A pig's orgasm lasts for 30 minutes. *(in my next life I want to be a pig!)*

• If you fart continuously for 6 years and 9 months, enough gas will be produced to create the energy of an atomic bomb.

• The male praying mantis cannot copulate while its head is attached to its body. The female initiates sex by ripping the males head off. *("Honey, I'm home. What the .....")*

• Some lions mate over 50 times a day.
(So it's PIG vs. LION : QUALITY vs. QUANTITY!)

SUMMARY: "Damn pigs!"

~~~~~~~~~~~~~~~~~~~~

**FOR SALE:
PARACHUTE**
Used Only Once;

Never Opened
(small stain)

Where do you find a dog
with no legs?

Right where you left him!

That's Stretching It A Bit!

There were two chaps who met every Friday in the pub. One was a Surgeon and the other a Handyman. The handyman used to boast that he could make something useful out of any thrown away material. So one day the surgeon, fed up with the handyman's boasting bet him £100 that he could bring him some discarded material which he would not be able to make anything useful out of. The bet was agreed to and the next week the surgeon turned up with a bag full of foreskins.

The following week the handyman turned up with a superbly crafted and sewn purse made from the foreskins with lots of internal pockets and zips all made from the same material.

The surgeon paid up and asked if he could take away the purse. Oh no said the handyman it will cost you more than that.

"What more than £100 for such a small purse?"

"Oh yes" replied the handyman but the beauty of this purse is that if you rub it hard enough it turns into a full size holdall for your holiday!"

~~~~~~~~~~~~~~~~~~~~

Taxi Driver

A naked woman flagged down a taxi driver late at night. When he arrived at her home he said to her "How are you going to pay?" She threw one leg over the right hand seat the other over the left hand seat and pointing in between her legs said "With this!" To which the taxi driver replied,

"Oh no haven't you got something smaller"

Fancy Dress

There's this man with a bald head and a wooden leg that gets invited to a fancy dress party.

He doesn't know what costume to wear to hide his head and his leg so he writes to a fancy dress company to explain the problem.

A few days later he receives a parcel with a note.
"Dear Sir, please find enclosed a pirates outfit. The spotted handkerchief will cover your bald head and with your wooden leg you will be just right as a pirate".

The man thinks this is terrible because they have just emphasised his wooden leg and so he writes a really rude letter of complaint.

A week passes and he receives another parcel and a note, which says "Dear Sir, sorry about before, please find enclosed a monks habit. The long robe will cover your wooden leg and with your bald head you will really look the part".

Now the man is really annoyed since they have gone from emphasising his wooden leg to emphasising his bald head and he writes the company a REALLY rude letter of complaint.

The next day he receives a small parcel and a note, which reads "Dear Sir, please find enclosed a tin of treacle.

INSTRUCTIONS:
Pour the tin of treacle over your bald head, stick your wooden leg up your arse and go as a toffee apple!"

Things Ain't What They Used To Be!

The old codgers were sitting by the fire while their young daughter and son-in law went up to bed. After they had been upstairs for a few minutes Ethel said to Bert. Pop up and have a look through the fanlight window and see what they are up to.

Bert did and came down and reported that they were playing quoits. The son-in-law was lying erect and the daughter was throwing quoits over his JT.

After a few more minutes Ethel asked Bert to go and have another look. He reported that now she was lying with her legs open and he was throwing peanuts into her fanny.

After a few more minutes Ethel said to Bert, "I would love to play that game."

"Alright," said Bert,
"I will pop down to Tesco's and get a pound of King Edwards."
And Ethel said, "I'll come with you and get a packet of Polos."

~~~~~~~~~~~~~~~~~~~~

Starkers in the Kitchen!

My next-door neighbour, John, he and his wife are naturists!
Always cavorting around at home with no clothes on at all!

Well, a few weeks back, what a calamity happened. John's wife
Carol was doing her stretching exercises in the kitchen, when she
did the splits, all the way down, and couldn't get up again! John
tried to help her up, but being a large woman, he couldn't move
her at all.
Well he knocked on my door and said, try not to be embarrassed,
but could I help him get her up off the kitchen floor as she's got
stuck doing the splits.
I went in to their kitchen and what a funny sight it was. He didn't
tell me she was starkers and it was all I could do not to laugh!

John said if we both get hold of an arm each, we could lift her up a
bit so she can get her legs going. Well we heaved hard and got her
up a bit but not enough. She said, "I'm still stuck to the floor".
Then we got hold of a buttock each, Christ, there was plenty to get
hold of too, and lifted her a couple of feet off the floor, but she
yelled out that her fanny was stuck to the floor. Well I bent down
to have a look and sure enough, there it was, stretched out like a
trumpet, stuck firmly to the tiles.
Christ it was a sight I couldn't believe.

I said to John, "I'm going to get a hammer and chisel to lift off the
tile that she's stuck to and then we'll get her up and put her in the
bath to soak the tile off".
Well, when I came back, John had got his hand on both her tits and
was massaging them furiously. I said, "What the hell are you doing
that for?"
He said, "I'm trying to get her sexed up a bit so we can slide her
over there to where the cheaper tiles are!"

Nursing Home Uses Viagra to Save Patient's Injury!

When Bert's wife died he was so upset he could not sleep, would not eat and was wasting away. His daughter heard about a nursing home and suggested that he go in for a few days to try it out.

He went in and after a few days he was looking great. His daughter asked him how things were. "Oh they're great," he replied. "Every evening the matron gives me two sleeping tablets and a Viagra and in the morning I feel fine."

The daughter went to see the matron and questioned her about the tablets her dad was getting. "Oh" said the matron, "these old boys are missing the sex and can't sleep, so I give them 2 sleeping tablets to make sure they get a good nights rest and 1 Viagra to make sure they don't roll out of bed.

~~~~~~~~~~~~~~~~~~~~~

A young boy approaches his mother and asks, "Why do women get married in white..?"

His Mother replies,
"Because females are angelic, virginal creatures and white is the colour of angels."

The boy asks his dad the same question, to which the father replies,

"All kitchen appliances are white, son."

When Nick met Stevie

Nick Faldo met Stevie Wonder at a concert and they got chatting and Stevie said, "Bet you didn't know I played golf, Nicky baby" "No I didn't" said Nick somewhat amazed, "apart from your obvious disability, do you have a handicap?"
"9 and falling!"
Nick said, "That's marvellous Stevie. I've got to ask, how do you manage to do that?"
"Well of course I have to have a little help. My bodyguard comes round with me and when I'm about to take a shot he selects my club for me and goes off in the direction I have to aim and whistles. And being blind I have super sensitive hearing and I am able to shoot exactly where the sound comes from!"
"That's bloody marvellous" said Nick. "How does it work when you get to the green?"
"Exactly the same" said Stevie, "the bodyguard stands behind the hole and whistles and I hardly ever 3 putt!"

"D'you fancy a game sometime Nick" said Stevie.
"Yeah that would be great" Nick replied.
"There is one thing" said Stevie, "I only ever play anyone for money."
"That's okay" said Nick "a side bet would be fun."
"Yeah man" said Stevie, "but I mean 100,000 dollars per hole." Nick thought this was too good to be true and said "Okay, whenever you like."
Stevie said, "Well I'm available any night next week!"

~~~~~~~~~~~~~~~~~~~~~

It Makes You Think.......

Why can't blondes fart?

Because they never stop talking long enough to build up any pressure.

~~~~~~~~~~~~~~~

Why does a dog lick it's balls?

Because it can!

~~~~~~~~~~~~~~~

What 's the definition of Trust?

Two cannibals giving each other a blow-job!

Picture Break

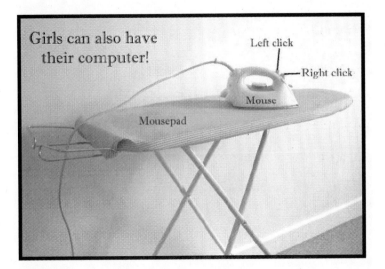

Picture Break

Gone,
but never to be forgotten

Picture Break

Picture Break

Authentic (allegedly)

Complaints Received by Local Councils from their Tenants:

I want some repairs done to my cooker as it has backfired and burnt my knob off.

I wish to complain that my father hurt his ankle very badly when he put his foot in the hole in his back passage.

Their 18 year old son is continuously banging his balls against my fence. Not only is this making a hell of a noise, but the fence is now sagging in the middle.

I wish to report that tiles are missing from the roof of the outside toilet and I think it was bad wind the other night that blew them off.

I request your permission to remove my drawers in the kitchen.

The toilet is blocked and we cannot bath the children until it is cleared.

Will you please send a man to look at my water, it is a funny colour and not fit to drink.

I want to complain about the farmer across the road; every morning at 5.30 his cock wakes me up and at my age it's too much.

My toilet seat is cracked – where do I stand?

The man next door has a large erection in the back garden, which is unsightly and dangerous.

Appraisal Compliments....

Try these more tasteful compliments.....
        ......for some of your less bright staff

- "Since my last report, he has reached rock bottom and has started to dig."

- He's not the sharpest knife in the drawer.

- "This employee is depriving a village somewhere of an idiot."

- "He would be out of his depth in a car park puddle."

- Got a full 6-pack, but lacks the plastic thingy to hold it all

    together.

- "This employee should go far - and the sooner he starts, the better."

- If you stand close enough to him you can hear the ocean.

- A gross ignoramus -144 times worse than an ordinary ignoramus.

- Gates are down, the lights are flashing, but the train isn't coming.

- It's hard to believe that he beat 1,000,000 other sperm out.

- "This young lady has delusions of adequacy."

- "She sets low personal standards and then consistently fails to achieve them."

Beer Turns Men into Women!

Yesterday, scientists for Health Canada suggested that men should take a look at their beer consumption, considering the results of a recent analysis that revealed the presence of female hormones in beer.

The theory is that drinking beer makes men turn into women.

To test the finding, 100 men were fed 6 pints of beer each.

It was then observed that 100% of the men gained weight, talked excessively without making sense, became overly emotional, couldn't drive, failed to think rationally, argued over nothing, and refused to apologise when wrong.

No further testing is planned.

~~~~~~~~~~~~~~~~~~~~~

The members of the executive board are all sitting round the boardroom table, with the chairman at the head of the table.

"Right Gentlemen," says the chairman, "the first item on the agenda, is to ask which one of you has NOT shagged my secretary."

There was a long hard silence, eventually one guy holds up his shaking hand.

So the chairman says "That's settled then, you go out and sack her"!

Top Chat-Up Lines

"Get your coat you've pulled"!

"Did you hurt yourself when you fell from heaven?"

"Is that a ladder in your tights or a stairway to heaven?"

What Does It Take to Change a Light Bulb?

How many THRILLER WRITERS does it take to change a light-bulb?
Two. One to screw it most of the way in and the other to give it a surprising twist at the end.

~~~~~~~~~~~~~~~~~~~~

How many PRISON WARDERS does it take to change a light-bulb?
Two. One screw to screw in the bulb and another screw to screw the first screw if he screws up.

~~~~~~~~~~~~~~~~~~~~

How many PESSIMISTS does it take to change a light-bulb?
"What's the point? It'll only blow again."

~~~~~~~~~~~~~~~~~~~~

How many FILM DIRECTORS does it take to change a light-bulb?
"I don't care how many it takes, what it costs, or how you do it - JUST GET IT CHANGED, OKAY?!?!!"

Men v. Women

Man :   would you sleep with me
              for £100...?
Woman : nope

Man :   £1000?
Woman : nope

Man :   £10,000?
Woman : nope

Man :   £100,000 ?
Woman : nope

Man :   £1,000,000?
Woman : mm....yes

Man :   OK, now we've established what you are, let's just
              haggle the price

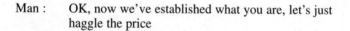

What's the similarity between a Woman and Kentucky Fried Chicken?

By the time you've finished with the breast and thighs, all you have left is a greasy box to pop your bone in!

Those Essex Girls
(Blondes in the US!)

On a plane bound for New York the flight attendant approached a blonde sitting in the first class section and requested that she move to economy since she did not have a first class ticket. The blonde replied "I'm blonde, I'm beautiful, I'm going to New York and I'm not moving."

Not wanting to argue with a customer, the flight attendant asked the co-pilot to speak with her. He went to talk with the woman asking her to please move out of the first class section.

Again, the blonde replied, "I'm blonde, I'm beautiful, I'm going to New York and I'm not moving." The co-pilot returned to the cockpit and asked the captain what he should do.

The captain said, "I'm married to a blonde, and I know how to handle this." He went to the first class section and whispered in the blonde's ear. She immediately jumped up and ran to the economy section mumbling to herself, "Why didn't anyone just say so?"

Surprised, the flight attendant and the co-pilot asked what he said to her that finally convinced her to move from her seat. He said, "I told her the first class section wasn't going to New York."

Actual Newspaper Headlines

IS THERE A RING OF DEBRIS AROUND URANUS?

~~~~~~~~~~~~~~~~~~~~~~~

DRUNK GETS NINE MONTHS IN VIOLIN CASE

~~~~~~~~~~~~~~~~~~~~~~~

SURVIVOR OF SIAMESE TWINS JOINS PARENTS

~~~~~~~~~~~~~~~~~~~~~~~

IRAQI HEAD SEEKS ARMS

Parcel Farce

Nelson Mandela is sitting at home watching the telly when he hears a knock at the door. When he opens it, he is confronted by a little Japanese man, clutching a clipboard and yelling, "You sign, you sign!"

Behind him is an enormous truck full of car exhausts.
Nelson is standing there in complete amazement when the Japanese man starts to yell louder.
"You sign! You sign!"

Nelson says to him, "Look mate, you've obviously got the wrong bloke. Get lost!" and shuts the door in the Japanese man's face.

The next day he hears a knock at the door again. When he opens it, the little Japanese man is back, with a huge truck full of brake pads. He thrusts his clipboard under Nelson's nose, yelling "You sign! You sign!"

Mr Mandela is getting a bit hacked off by now, so he shoves the little Japanese man back, shouting:
"Look, get lost!! You've got the wrong bloke! I don't want them!" then slams the door in the Japanese man's face again.

The following day Nelson is resting, and late in the afternoon, hears a knock on the door again. Upon opening the door, the little Japanese man thrusts the same clipboard under his nose, shouting "You sign! You sign!"
Behind him are TWO large trucks full of wing mirrors.

Nelson loses his temper completely, picks the little man up by his shirt front and yells at him, "Look, I don't want these! Do you understand? You must have the wrong man!
Who do you want to give these to?" The little Japanese man looks at him a bit puzzled, consults his clipboard,
And says:
"You not Nissan Maindealer?"

More Ways to Change a Light Bulb!

How many WAITERS does it take to change a light-bulb?
None. Even a burned-out bulb can't catch a waiter's eye.

~~~~~~~~~~~~~~~~~~~~~~~~~~~~~

How many NUDISTS does it take to change a light-bulb?
Two. It only takes one to change the bulb, but it takes
another one to hand him up the new bulb because the first
one has nowhere to put it while he climbs the ladder.

~~~~~~~~~~~~~~~~~~~~~~~~~~~~~

How many BUS DRIVERS does it take to change a
light-bulb?
You've got to be joking - they won't even change a
five-pound note.

~~~~~~~~~~~~~~~~~~~~~~~~~~~~~

How many VENTRILOQUISTS does it take to change a
light-bulb?
Two. One to change the gulg and one to gold the gottom of
the lagger.

~~~~~~~~~~~~~~~~~~~~~~~~~~~~~

How many TEENAGERS does it take to change a
light-bulb?
"Do it yourself - it's your house! What am I, some kind of
personal slave or something?"

WEEKEND ALCOHOL WARNING

Due to increasing products liability litigation alcohol manufacturers have accepted the Medical Association's suggestion that the following warning labels be placed immediately on all alcohol containers:

WARNING Consumption of alcohol may make you think you are whispering when you are not.

WARNING Consumption of alcohol is a major factor in dancing like a plonker.

WARNING Consumption of alcohol may cause you to tell the same boring story over and over again until your friends want to SMASH YOUR HEAD IN.

WARNING Consumption of alcohol may lead you to believe that ex-lovers are really dying for you to telephone them at 4 in the morning.

WARNING Consumption of alcohol may leave you wondering what the hell happened to your trousers.

WARNING Consumption of alcohol may think you can converse logically with members of the opposite sex without spitting.

WARNING Consumption of alcohol may cause you to roll over in the morning and see something really scary *(whose species or name you cannot remember)*.

WARNING Consumption of alcohol is the leading cause of inexplicable rug burns on the forehead.

WARNING Consumption of alcohol may create the illusion that you are tougher, more handsome and smarter than some really, really big guy named Dave.

WARNING Consumption of alcohol may lead you to believe fat, ugly people are slim and attractive.

WARNING Consumption of alcohol may lead to traffic signs and cones appearing in your home.

WARNING Consumption of alcohol may lead you to believe that people are laughing WITH you.

Shorties

In Flight Attendant's Announcement:

Weather at our destination is 50 degrees with some broken clouds, but they'll try to have them fixed before we arrive.

~~~~~~~~~~~~~~~~~~~~

One tequila, two tequila, three tequila, floor.

~~~~~~~~~~~~~~~~~~~~

What do Monica Lewinsky and a Coke machine have in common?

They both have slots saying "Enter Bill face up"

~~~~~~~~~~~~~~~~~~~~

Genie

A couple are golfing one day on a very, very exclusive golf course lined with million dollar houses. On the third tee the husband says, "Honey, be very careful when you drive the ball. Don't knock out any windows? It'll cost us a fortune to fix."

The wife tees up and promptly shanks it right through the window of the biggest house on the course. The husband cringes and says, "I told you to watch out for the houses! All right, let's go up there, apologise and see how much this is going to cost."

They walk up and knock, and a voice says, "Come in." When they open the door, they see glass all over the floor and a broken bottle lying on its side in the foyer. A man on the couch says, "Are you the people that broke my window?"
"Uh, yeah," the husband says. "Sorry about that."
"No, actually I want to thank you. I'm a genie that was trapped for a thousand years in that bottle. You've released me. I'm allowed to grant three wishes? I'll give you each one wish, and I'll keep the last one for myself."

"OK, great!" the husband says. "I want a million dollars a year for the rest of my life."
"No problem? It's the least I could do. And you, what do you want?" the genie says, looking at the wife.
"I want a house in every country of the world," she says.
"Consider it done."

"And what's your wish, Genie?" the husband asks.
"Well, since I've been trapped in that bottle, I haven't had sex with a woman in a thousand years. My wish is to sleep with your wife."

The husband looks at the wife and says, "Well, we did get a lot of money and all those houses, honey. I guess it's OK with me if it's OK with you."

So the genie takes the wife upstairs and ravishes her for two hours. Afterward, he rolls over, looks at the wife, and says, "How old is your husband, anyway?"
"35. Why?"

"And he still believes in genies?"

65

A Few of our Favourite
TV Gaffes!

"This is really a lovely horse, I once rode her mother."
(Ted Walsh - Horse Racing Commentator)

"He's pulling him off! The Spanish Manager is pulling his captain off!" *(RTE's George Hamilton on Spain Manager Luis Suarez's substitution of Butragueno during their world cup qualifier with Ireland in Seville, 1992)*

~~~~~~~~~~~~~~~~~~~~~

"I never comment on referees and I'm not going to break the habit of a lifetime for that prat." *(Ron Atkinson 1997)*

~~~~~~~~~~~~~~~~~~~~~

"Ah, isn't that nice, the wife of the Cambridge president is kissing the cox of the Oxford crew." *(Harry Carpenter - BBC TV Boat Race 1977)*

~~~~~~~~~~~~~~~~~~~~~

"And for those of you who watched the last programme (Fanny and Johnny Craddock), I hope all your doughnuts turn out like Fanny's." *(David Coleman at the start of Match of The Day)*

~~~~~~~~~~~~~~~~~~~~~

"One of the reasons Arnie (Arnold Palmer) is playing so well is that,before each tee-shot, his wife takes out his balls and kisses them - Oh my God, what have I just said?" *(USTV commentator Johnny Huntridge)*

~~~~~~~~~~~~~~~~~~~~~

Ee aw ee aw ee aw
to know better

What do you call a donkey with one leg?
A wonky donkey.

What do you call a donkey with one leg and one eye?
A winky wonky donkey.

What do you call a donkey with one leg and one eye makin' love?
A bonky winky wonky donkey.

What do you call a donkey with one leg and one eye makin' love while breaking wind?
A stinky bonky winky wonky donkey.

What do you call a donkey with one leg and one eye makin' love while breaking wind, wearing blue suede shoes?
A honky tonky stinky bonky winky wonky donkey.

What do you call a donkey with one leg and one eye makin' love while breaking wind, wearing blue suede shoes and playing piano?
A plinky plonky honky tonky stinky bonky winky wonky donkey.

~~~~~~~~~~~~~~~~~~~~

*Age
is a very high price
to pay for maturity*

**THE OLDER YOU GET,
THE BETTER YOU
REALISE
YOU WERE**

Do You Have What It Takes to Join the CIA?

A few months ago, there was an opening with the CIA for an assassin. After sending some applicants through the background checks, training and testing, they narrowed the possible choices down to 3 men, but only one position was available.

The day came for the final test to see which man would get the extremely secretive job.
The CIA men administering the test took one of the men to a large metal door and handed him a gun. "We must know that you will follow your instructions no matter what the circumstances", they explained.
"Inside this room, you will find your wife sitting in a chair. Take this gun and kill her."
The man got a shocked look on his face and said "You can't be serious! I could never shoot my own wife!" "Well", says the CIA man, "you're definitely not the right man for this job then."

So they bring the second man to the same door and hand him a gun. "We must know that you will follow instructions no matter what the circumstances", they explained to the second man. "Inside you will find your wife sitting in a chair. Take this gun and kill her."

The second man looked a bit shocked, but nevertheless took the gun and went into the room. All was quiet for about 5 minutes, then the door opened. The man came out of the room with tears in his eyes. "I tried to shoot her, I just couldn't pull the trigger and shoot my wife. I guess I'm not the right man for the job." "No" the CIA man replied, "You don't have what it takes. Take your wife and go the hell home."

Now they're down to one man left to test. Again they lead him to the same door to the same room and hand him the same gun. "We must be sure that you will follow instructions no matter what the circumstances, this is your final test. Inside you will find your wife sitting in a chair. Take this gun and kill her." The third man took the gun and opened the door. Before the door even closed all the way, the CIA man heard the gun start firing. One shot after another for 13 shots. Then all hell broke loose in the room. They heard screaming, crashing, banging on the walls. This went on for several minutes, then all went quiet. The door opened slowly, and there stood the third man. He wiped the sweat from his brow and said "You guys didn't tell me the gun was loaded with blanks! I had to beat the bitch to death with the f*ck*ng chair!"

Essential Guide for all Wives & Would Be Wives

This is a true extract from a Home Economics textbook printed in the early 60s. Absolutely unbelievable! Men love it. Women can't believe it actually existed.

The Good Wives' Guide

Have dinner ready. Plan ahead, even the night before, to have a delicious meal ready on time for his return home from work. This is a way of letting him know that you have been thinking about him and are concerned about his needs. Most men are hungry when they come home and the prospect of a good meal (especially his favourite dish) is part of the warm welcome needed.

Prepare yourself. Take 15 minutes to rest so you will be refreshed when he arrives. Touch up your make-up, put a ribbon in your hair and be fresh looking. He has just been with a lot of work weary people. Be a little gay and a little more interesting for him. His boring day may need a lift and one of your duties is to provide it.

Clear away the clutter. Make one last trip through the main part of the house just before your husband arrives. Gather up schoolbooks, toys, papers, etc. and the run a dustcloth over the tables. Over the cooler months of the year you should prepare and light a fire for him to unwind by. Your husband will feel he has reached a haven of rest and order and it will give you a lift too. After all, catering for his comfort will provide you with immense personal satisfaction. Minimise all noise. At the time of his arrival, eliminate all noise of the washer, dryer or vacuum.

Try to encourage the children to be quiet. Be happy to see him. Greet him with a warm smile and show sincerity in your desire to please him. Listen to him. You may have a dozen important things to tell him, but the moment of his arrival is not the time. Let him talk first, remember, his topics of conversation are more important than yours. Make the evening his. Never complain if he comes home late or goes out to dinner, or other places of entertainment without you. Instead, try to understand his world of strain and pressure and his very real need to be at home and relax.

Your goal: Try to make sure your home is a place of peace, order and tranquillity where your husband can renew himself in body and spirit. Don't greet him with complaints and problems. Don't complain if he's late home for dinner, or even stays out all night. Count this as minor compared to what he might have gone through that day.

Make him comfortable. Have him lean back in a comfortable chair or have him lie down in the bedroom. Have a cool or warm drink ready for him. Arrange the pillow and offer to take off his shoes. Speak in a low, soothing and pleasant voice. Don't ask him questions about his actions or question his judgement or integrity. Remember, he is the master of the house and as such will always exercise his will with fairness and truthfulness.

THE GIRLIES PRAYER

Our Marks
Which art with Spencers
Hallowed be thy food hall
Thy Gucci watch
Thy Kookai bag
In Hermes
As it is in Harrods
Give us each day our Visa Gold
And forgive us our overdraft
As we forgive those who stop our Next Card
And lead us not into Dorothy Perkins
And deliver us from Topshop
For thine is the Naff Naff, The Cartier and the Versace
For Gaultier and Eternity
AMEX

THE LADS' PRAYER

Our beer,
Which art in barrels,
Hallowed be thy drink.
Thy will be drunk,
I will be drunk,
At home as it is in the local.
Forgive us this day our daily spillage
As we forgive those who spillest
against us.
And lead us not into the practice of
poncy wine tasting,
And deliver us from alcopops,
For mine is the bitter,
the ale and the lager,
Forever and ever;
BARMEN

~~~~~~~~~~~~~~~~~~~~

INDIAN CHARTS - TOP 20

1. Bhaji Trousers – Madness
2. Bhuna to be Wild – Steppenwolf
3. Bye Bye Balti – Bay City Rollers
4. Love me Tandoor – Elvis Presley
5. Tandoor Deliver – Adam and the Ants

6. Livin' Dhal – Cliff Richard
7. Vindaloo – Abba
8. Dansak on the Ceiling – Lionel Richie
9. Bhuna Round The World and I Can't Find My Balti – Lisa Stansfield
10. Take That and Chapati – Take That
11. It's My Chapati and I Cry If I Want To –- Dave Stewart/Barbara Gaskin
12. Korma Chameleon – Culture Club
13. Brothers in Naans – Dire Straits
14. It's Bhuna Hard Days Night – The Beatles
15. Tears On My Pilau – Kylie Minogue
16. Things Can Only Get Bhuna – D:Ream
17. You Can't Curry Love – Diana Ross and the Supremes
18. When I Phal in Love – Nat King Cole
19. Tikka Chance On Me – Abba
20. Dansak Queen – Abba

Poetry In Motion

Grant me the serenity to accept the things I
cannot change,
The courage to change the things I cannot
accept,
And the wisdom to hide the bodies of those
people I had to kill today because they pissed
me off.

And also, help me to be careful
Of the toes I step on today
As they may be connected
To the ass that I may have to kiss tomorrow.

Help me to always give 100% at work...
12% on Monday,
23% on Tuesday,
40% on Wednesday,
20% on Thursday and
5% on Fridays.

And help me to remember...
When I'm having a really bad day,
And it seems that people are trying to piss me
off,
That it takes 42 muscles to frown
And only 4 to extend my middle finger

Men v. Women

To make love,
Women need a reason,
Men need a place

~~~~~~~~~~~~~~~~~~~~

If a man is standing in the middle of the forest speaking and there is no woman around to hear him...is he still wrong?

~~~~~~~~~~~~~~~~~~~~

Men are from Earth, Women are from Earth.
Deal with it.

~~~~~~~~~~~~~~~~~~~~

Women like silent men; they think they're listening.

Men like Silence; they don't have to listen.

~~~~~~~~~~~~~~~~~~~~

TEN BEST THINGS TO SAY IF YOU GET CAUGHT SLEEPING AT YOUR DESK:

10. "They told me at the blood bank this might happen."

9. "This is just a 15 minute power-nap like they raved about in that time management course you sent me to."

8. "Whew! Guess I left the top off the liquid paper. You probably got here just in time!"

7. "I wasn't sleeping! I was meditating on the mission statement and envisioning a new paradigm."

6. "I was testing my keyboard for drool resistance."

5. "I was doing a highly specific Yoga exercise to relieve work-related stress.
Are you discriminatory toward people who practice Yoga?"

4. "Damn! Why did you interrupt me?
I had almost figured out a solution to our biggest problem."

3. "The coffee machine is broken..."

2. "Someone must've put decaf in the wrong pot..."

1. " ... Amen."

HOW TO SHOWER LIKE A MAN

Short version:
1. Take off clothes while sitting on the edge of the bed and leave them in a pile on the floor.

2. Walk to bathroom wearing a towel. If you see your girlfriend/wife along the way, flash her.

3. Look at your manly physique in the mirror and suck in your gut to see if you have pecs. (no)

4. Turn on the water.

5. Check for pecs again. (no)

6. Get in the shower.

7. Don't bother to look for a washcloth. (you don't use one)

8. Wash your face.

9. Wash your armpits.

10. Wash your penis and surrounding area.

11. Wash your ass.

12. Shampoo your hair. (do not use conditioner)

13. Make a shampoo Mohawk.

14. Open the door and look at yourself in the mirror.

15. Pee

16. Rinse off and get out of the shower.

17. Return to the bedroom wearing a towel, if you pass your girlfriend/wife, flash her.

HOW TO SHOWER LIKE A WOMAN

Long version: (sorry, there is no short version with women)

1. Take off the fourteen layers of clothing you put on this morning because there was a distinct chill in the air due to the temperature dropping below 33 degrees.

2. Walk to bathroom wearing long dressing gown and towel on head. If you see your boyfriend/husband along the way, cover up any exposed flesh immediately, ignore his juvenile turban gags and then rush to bathroom.

3. Look at your womanly physique in the mirror and stick out your gut so that you can complain and whine even more about how you're getting fat.

4. Turn on the hot water only.

5. Get in the shower, once you have found it through all that steam.

6. Look for facecloth, armcloth, legcloth, long loofah, wide loofah and pumice stone.

7. Wash your hair once with Cucumber and Lamfrey shampoo with 83 added vitamins.

8. Wash your hair again with Cucumber and Lamfrey shampoo with 83 added vitamins.

9. Wash your hair once more with Cucumber and Lamfrey shampoo with 83 added vitamins.

10. Condition your hair with Cucumber and Lamfrey conditioner enhanced with natural crocus oil. Leave on hair for fifteen minutes.

11. Wash your face with crushed apricot facial scrub for ten minutes until red raw.

12. Wash entire rest of body with Ginger Nut and Jaffa Cake bodywash.

13. Complain bitterly when you realize that your boyfriend/husband has once again been eating your Ginger Nut and Jaffa Cake body wash.

14. Rinse conditioner off hair (this takes at least fifteen minutes as you must make sure that it has all come off).

15. Debate shaving armpits and legs and decide that you can't be bothered, and anyway the hair helps keep you warm.

16. Slick hair back and pretend you're like Bo Derek in 10.

17. Scream loudly when your boyfriend/husband flushes the toilet and you get a rush of cold water.

18. Turn hot water on full and rinse off.

19. Dry with a towel the size of a small African country.

20. Check entire body for the remotest sign of a spot. Attack with nails/tweezers if found.

21. Return to bedroom wearing long dressing gown and towel on head. If you see your boyfriend/husband along the way, cover up any exposed flesh immediately, ignore his juvenile turban gags and then rush to bedroom.

Got Any Samples?

Old Bert, was nearly 85, and not feeling that well, so his missus took him off to the Doctor one day.

Old Bert was quite Mutt and Jeff these days, so his missus would answer most of the questions for him.

As Dr. Jones was examining him, he said "You're not doing bad for your age, Bert".
"What'd he say?" yelled Bert at his missus.
"You're not bad yer silly 'ole bugger" she yelled at him.

"What are his symptoms" the doctor asked Bert's missus.
"It's painful to go to the toilet" she told him.

The doctor thought and said "I'm going to need some samples of his Urine, Stools and Semen, if possible; could you manage that?" he said to her.

"What'd he say?" yelled Bert again at his missus.

"He says he wants to examine your pyjamas" she yelled back.

The Gates of Heaven or Hell?

Bill Gates died in a car accident. He found himself in Purgatory being sized up by God.

"Well, Bill, I'm really confused on this call. I'm not sure whether to send you to Heaven or Hell. After all, you enormously helped society by putting a computer in almost every home in the world and yet you created that ghastly Windows 95. I'm going to do something I've never done before.

In your case, I'm going to let you decide where you want to go!"

Bill replied, "Well, thanks, God. What's the difference between the two?"

God said, "I'm willing to let you visit both places briefly if it will help you make a decision."

"Fine, but where should I go first?"

God said, "I'm going to leave that up to you."

Bill said, "OK, then, let's try Hell first."

So Bill went to hell. It was a beautiful, clean, sandy beach with clear waters. There were thousands of beautiful women running around, playing in the water, laughing and frolicking about. The sun was shining. The temperature was perfect. Bill was very pleased.

"This is great!" he told God. "If this is Hell, I REALLY want to see Heaven!"

Fine," said God and off they went. Heaven was a high place in the clouds with angels drifting about playing harps and singing. It was nice, but not as enticing as Hell. Bill thought for a quick minute and rendered his decision.

"Hmm, I think I prefer Hell" he told God.

"Fine," retorted God, "as you desire." So Bill Gates went to Hell.

Two weeks later, God decided to check up on the late billionaire to see how he was doing in Hell. When God arrived in Hell, he found Bill shackled to a wall, screaming amongst the hot flames in a dark cave. He was being burned and tortured by demons.

"How's everything going, Bill?" God asked.

Bill responded - his voice full of anguish and disappointment, "This is awful, this is not what I expected. I can't believe this happened. What happened to that other place with the beaches and the beautiful women playing in the water?"

God said "Oh, that was just the screen saver."

Perfect Fairy Tale

Once upon a time, a perfect man and a perfect woman met. After a perfect courtship, they had a perfect wedding. Their life together was, of course, perfect.

One snowy, stormy Christmas Eve, this perfect couple were driving their perfect car along a winding road, when they noticed someone at the side of the road in distress. Being the perfect couple, they stopped to help.

There stood Santa Claus with a huge bundle of toys. Not wanting to disappoint any children on the eve of Christmas, the perfect couple loaded Santa and his toys into their vehicle. Soon they were driving along delivering the toys.

Unfortunately, the driving conditions deteriorated and the perfect couple and Santa Claus had an accident. Only one of them survived the accident.

Who was the survivor? (look down for the answer.)

The perfect woman. She's the only one who really existed in the first place.
Everyone knows there is no Santa Claus and there is no such thing as a perfect man.

Women, end story here.

Men, turn the page.

...Perfect Fairy Tale ~ continued.......

So, if there is no perfect man and no Santa Claus, the perfect woman must have been driving. This explains why there was a car accident.

By the way, if you're a woman and you're reading this, this brings up another point: women are incapable of following even the simplest of instructions !!

~~~~~~~~~~~~~~~~~~~~~

More Shorties

<u>How can you tell if your wife is dead?</u>
The Sex is the same, but the dishes pile up.

<u>How do you annoy your girlfriend during sex?</u>
Phone Her.

<u>What's the difference between Oral and Anal
Sex?</u>
Oral Sex makes your day.
Anal sex makes your hole weak!

<u>Woman's definition of Oral Sex:</u>
Something you used to do to your man before you got
married.

<u>How can you make 5 pounds of fat look good?</u>
Put a nipple on it!

Noah's New Ark!

Noah, get's called into the office to see God one day, and God tells him he wants him to build another ark. Noah asks why as there was nothing wrong with the first one.

God replies, 'It's nothing like I asked for. I didn't ask you to make one in which other creatures can be safe. Please build a floating aquarium with three floors.
This time it will be exclusively for fish. The big fish can go downstairs and the smaller ones can go in the middle and the delicate tropical fishes can go on the upper deck.'

Noah thought long and hard about this one but finally said,

"Am I correct in thinking that what you want is a multi-storey Carp Ark'?"

~~~~~~~~~~~~~~~~~~~~

How can you tell if your Valentine is from a Leper?

The tongue is still in the envelope!

Some More Quickies!

- A lady walks into the local hardware store and says
  "I need a hinge please?"
  The guy behind the counter says
  "Do you wanna screw for the hinge"
  "No, but I'll blow yer for a toaster!"

- *Did you hear about the Jewish Kamikaze Pilot?*
  Crashed his plane into his brother's scrap yard!

- How many screws in a Lesbian's coffin?
  None! It's all tongue and groove!

- **Why did God invent alcohol?**
  So ugly girls could get laid too!

- How do you stop a woman performing oral sex?
  Marry Her!

- **A man was watching a dog lick its balls. He said to its owner "I wish I could do that!**
- **He replied "Give him a biscuit and he'll let you!"**

Aim Low,
Reach your Goals,
Avoid Disappointment

~~~~~~~~~~~~~~~~~~~~

HANG IN THERE; RETIREMENT IS ONLY FIFTY YEARS AWAY!

~~~~~~~~~~~~~~~~~~~~

PLAGIARISM SAVES TIME

~~~~~~~~~~~~~~~~~~~~~

Doing a job RIGHT the first time gets the job done. Doing the job WRONG fourteen times gives you job security.

Subject: Great being a man...1

Understanding rugby, football, cricket, baseball, American football – in fact any game called football.

A five day holiday requires one overnight bag.

Phone conversations are over in 30 seconds flat.

Queues for the bathroom don't exist.

You can open all your own jars.

When clicking through the channels you don't have to pause at every shot of someone crying.

All your orgasms are real.

You don't have to lug a bag of useless stuff around.

You can go to the bathroom without a support group.

When your work is criticised, you understand that everyone doesn't secretly hate you.

You get extra credit for the slightest act of thoughtfulness.

Nobody wonders if you swallow.

You never have to clean a toilet.

You can shower, shit, shave and ready to go in 10 minutes.

You save time and money by washing up in bulk every third week.

Sex means never worrying about your reputation. In fact it makes it.

Receiving blow jobs.

Wedding plans take care of themselves.

If someone forgets to invite you to something, it means that they forgot to invite you. It doesn't mean that they hate you. Also he or she can still be your friend.

You don't have to shave below your neck.

None of your co-workers have the power to make you cry.

You don't have to curl up next to a hairy butt every night.

If you're over 27 and single, nobody even notices.

You can write your name in the snow.

Just Like That! – (for Tommy Cooper fans)

My daughter answered the door the other day. She came in and said, Dad, there's a man at the door with a bald head.
I said "Tell him I've already got one!"

I rang up a local building firm, I said "I want a skip outside my house." He said "Go Ahead, I'm not stopping you."

Subject: Great being a man...2

Chocolate is just another snack.

Flowers fix everything.

You never have to worry about other people's feelings.

You get to think about sex 90% of your waking hours.

You can eat a banana in a hardware store.

Reverse parking is easy.

Foreplay is optional.

Window shopping is what you do when you buy windows.

Michael Bolton does not exist in your universe.

You don't have to clean your house if the meter reader's coming by.

You never feel compelled to stop a pal from getting laid. In fact you encourage them.

Car mechanics tell you the truth.

You don't give a rat's arse if no-one notices your new haircut.

You can quietly watch a game on TV with a buddy for hours without ever thinking he's mad at you.

The whole world is your urinal.

One mood, all the time.

Grey hair and wrinkles add character.
No such thing as bunny-hopping half an inch above the toilet seat.

People never glance at your chest when you're talking to them.

If you don't call your buddy when you say you will, he won't tell your other friends and they won't try and work out what the problem is. Nor imagine one if one does not exist.

Someday you'll be a dirty old man. And you're looking forward to it.

Porn movies are designed specifically with your mind in mind.

Not liking a person doesn't exclude having great sex with them.

Farts are not just funny, they are bloody hilarious

KNOCK KNOCK

Knock Knock on the front door.

Important looking gent says "Are you Bert Higginbotham?"
"Yes I am"
"I'm from the Ministry of War and I've come to award you compensation for your injuries received in the Second World War."
"That's 50 years ago! You've come to apologise for my injuries suffered 50 years ago?!!!!!" screamed Bert
"You cheeky Bastard! Compensation! 50 years late!"

"Right!" continued Bert, "I'll take compensation in the form of £1 per inch from the tip of my cock all the way to my bollocks"

"If that's what will make you happy" said the man from London.

"Aye, it bloody will," said Bert, already undoing his kegs.
Right, get ruler lad. Here we go.
"From the tip of me cock, 1 – 2 – 3 – 4 – 5."
"Excuse me Sir", said the important War man, "but where are your balls?"

"On the fucking beach at Dunkirk!"

The Kind Pet Shop Man

The Old Lady lived on her own and only had her cat for company.
Sadly, one day it got run over.

Distraught, the old lady went to the kind man in the Pet Shop and
asked what he had that would make a nice pet to keep her company.
"How about a talking canary" he asked? "It's the last one and the very
best I have." "Alright young man, how much is it?"
"£20 for the bird and £20 for the cage" Okay
she said and paid him the money.

After 5 days the canary had not said a thing so
the old lady went back to the Pet Shop and told
the kind man.

After
Dinner
CLASSIC!

"So, with your face up to his cage, you talk to
him? "Yes" she said "and then he runs up his
ladder......." "I haven't got a ladder" said the
old lady. Oh he said "Here's one, that'll be a fiver."

Off she went but after another 5 days she was back again, claiming he
still had not spoken.
"So, with your face up to his cage, you talk to him, he runs up his
ladder, looks in the mirror......." "I haven't got a mirror" said the old
lady.
Oh he said "Here's one, that'll be a fiver."

Off she went but after another 5 days she was back again, claiming
he still had not spoken.
"So, with your face up to his cage, you talk to him, he runs up his
ladder, looks in the mirror, rings the bell......." "I haven't got a bell"
said the old lady.
Oh he said "Here's one, that'll be a fiver."

Off she went but after another 5 days she was back again, looking
very sad. "What's the matter" said the Pet Shop man.

"Well I was talking to him, and he ran up his ladder, looked in the
mirror, rang the bell, said seven words, and dropped down dead.

"What did he say" said the Pet Shop Man.
Oh he said, "For fucks sake get me some seed."

Don't Mess with the F.B.I.

Young Billie Jo was new in the army and while camped out in the desert of the Wild West, he became ill and asked his Sergeant if he could see the Doctor.

"Doctor!" barked the Sergeant. "You're in the army now boy, the guy that makes you better is called the M.O. and you'd better start learning the army language."

A week later, the army camped up outside a local Western town, and Billie Jo was in the saloon and, missing the delights of female company, asked one of his more senior colleagues where the "action" was around there.

After Dinner CLASSIC!

"What you need to do Billie Jo is this" he said.

"Go to the I.R.

Find an I.S.

Take her to a W.W.

And give her a G.P."

"That's great" said Billie Jo, "but what the fuck are you talkin' about?"

"Go to the I.R. (Indian Reservation), find an I.S.(Indian Squaw), take her to a W.W.(Wig Wam) and give her a G.P.(Good Portion)."

So 2 weeks later when Billie Jo had a few days leave, off he went in search of some action.

The following day, he staggered into the local saloon, with a black eye, broken arm, and swollen face.

"Hey what happened to you" his mates cried. "we thought you were off to the I.R. to find an I.S., take her to a W.W. and give her a G.P?

"Well I went to the I.R., found a lovely I.S., went back to her W.W. and was just giving her a G.P. when the F.B.I. came in."

"What, the Federal Bureau of Investigation?"

"No" said Billie Jo, a "Fucking Big Indian!"

The Silver Caddy

After Dinner CLASSIC!

Gordon went into the Pro shop one afternoon at a new golf course and asked if there was anybody waiting for a game with whom he could pair up.
"No" said the pro, "its really quiet today."
"Oh that's a real shame" said Gordon, "I've got some new clubs and really wanted to give them their first outing."

"Well I'll tell you what I could do", said the Pro. "This is not meant to be used yet, as it's not been properly tested, but if you wish, I'll let you have it for nothing, if you'll give me a report on it when you come in."
"What is it?" asked Gordon.
"It's a Robot Caddy" said the Pro, proudly wheeling out a splendid Silver & White robot.
"We have programmed it using GSP and it will tell you from exactly where you are, how far it is to the pin, any hazards to watch out for and it will suggest which club you should use. Have fun!"

Sceptically, Gordon wheeled the robot to the first tee. The robot suddenly spoke,
"386 yards to the pin; Use a driver, aim up the left of the fairway."
Gordon was amazed, but did as suggested and hit a good shot. At the point where the ball landed, the robot said "154 yards to the pin; use a 6 iron and aim left of the pin". Gordon again followed instructions, and the ball he hit pitched left of the pin but rolled right up to the pin making use of the borrow. Fantastic!

Gordon's round continued with the robot highlighting all the hidden ditches and borrows on the greens and Gordon had become friendly with the robot and was seen chatting away to it on his way back to the clubhouse.
The Pro met him and Gordon regaled him with the astounding news and a score of 64 gross, his best ever, especially off a 24 handicap!

About 6 months went by before Gordon returned to this club and he asked the pro if the robot was available to accompany him today.

The Pro looked sad. He said, "We don't have it any longer."

"Why Not?!" demanded Gordon, "It was Brilliant!"

"Ah" said the Pro, "You'll remember that it was predominantly white with Silver?" "Yes" said Gordon. "Well during the summer we had lots of complaints from members saying it glinted so much in the sunshine out on the course that it was putting them off their game, so we painted it black."

"So where is it now" asked Gordon.

"We had to get rid of it, I'm afraid. No sooner we painted it black than it started coming in late, things went missing, it started playing loud music, the till wouldn't balance....................."

~~~~~~~~~~~~~~~~~~~~~~~~~~

Yesterday is history.
Tomorrow's a mystery.
Today is a gift.
That's why it's called the Present!

~~~~~~~~~~~~~~~~~~~~~~~~~~

Monty was guesting for Charity with a friend at the local deaf and dumb Golf Club when a golf ball smacked him in the back of the head.

Angrily he looked round to see who had not yelled out FORE! when he saw a golfer holding four fingers in the air.

It's a Custard Story.........

A New Yorker decides to have a party and invites lots of people, telling them, to bring their friends. On the invitation he puts "Theme party — come as a human emotion."

On the night of the party his first guest arrives and he opens the door to see a guy covered in green paint with the letters N and V painted on his chest.
He says to this guy "Wow, great outfit, what have you come as?" and the guy says, "I'm green with envy" and the host replies "Brilliant, come on in and have a drink."

A few minutes later the next guest arrives and the host opens the door to see a woman covered in a pink bodystocking with a feather boa wrapped round her most intimate parts. He says to this woman. "Wow, great outfit, what emotion have you come as?" And she replies, "I'm tickled pink". The host says, "I love it. Come on in and join the party."

A couple of minutes later the doorbell goes for the third time and the host opens the door to see two guys, stark naked, one with his penis stuck in a bowl of custard and the other with his penis stuck in a pear. The host is really shocked and says, "Christ guys, what the hell do you think you look like? You could get arrested for standing like that out here in the street. What emotion is this supposed to be?"
The first guy replies, "Well I'm fucking disgusted and my friend here has come in despair."

Name That Child!

An Englishman, Irishman and Scotsman were discussing children's names over a pint one day.

The Scotsman said
"My son was born on St. Andrew's Day so we were proud to name him Andrew."

The Englishman said
"My son was born on St. George's Day so we too were very proud to name him George."

The Irishman said
"Bejesus, that's a grand co-incidence to be sure. That exactly how my boy Pancake got his name too!"

Mac - The Apple Inventor

Mac was a bit of an inventor and was often at the Patent Office with his latest concoction, but today he knew he had something really special.
The Patent's Inspector said, "Okay Mac, what have you got for me today then"?
"An APPLE" beamed Mac.
"Apples have been around since Adam" sighed the Inspector.
"Not this variety" said Mac "Here, take a bite."

"Ugh!" Said the Inspector, "it tastes like Strawberries."
"Turn it round" said Mac.
"Hey this tastes like Blackcurrants"
"Turn it round" said Mac.
"Its Bananas round here" said the Inspector
Turn it round" said Mac.
"And this is a fig" he said, startled.
"Exactly" said Mac. What an invention eh?"
After some deep thought, the Patents Inspector said, "Good try Mac, but I don't think you can market this. I mean why would people want a mixed fruit apple, when they can already buy these separately? Maybe you should come up with one that tastes like a woman's fanny!" he joked. "That'd be a winner!"

Two months later, Mac was back!
"You know you mentioned I'd have a winner if I could invent a apple that tastes like a woman's fanny?" he said to the Inspector. "Well try this!"
"Errrrgggghhh! It tastes like shit" yelled the Inspector.
"Turn it round" beamed Mac.

MATHS AND LOGIC !

Two guys are chatting in a pub.

"How's your lad getting on ?" says one. "Went to University didn't he?"

After Dinner CLASSIC!

"That's right," says the proud father. "He's studying Maths and Logic".

"Well I know what Maths is" says the first bloke, "But what the fuck is logic?"

"I'll explain it to you," says the other guy. "You've got a fish tank at home, right?"

"Right," says the first guy. "So you must like fish."

"Yeah I love 'em. Sit and watch 'em swimming around for hours."

"And if you like fish, then its logical that you like animals."

"Oh yeah." says the first guy. We've got dogs, cats – I love animals."

"And if you like animals, it's logical that you like people," says the father.

"Oh yeah," says the first guy. "Our house is always full of friends and relatives."

"And if you like people, it stands to reason that you like women."

"Oh yes, I do like the ladies" says the first bloke.

"And if you like women, then it is logical to assume that you like sex."
Continues the father.

"Not 'arf! As much as I can get."

"Well there you are," says the father, "That is a string of logic."

The father goes off for his lunch and the first bloke is joined by another mate.

"I've just been talking to old Harry." he says to the newcomer. "His son is at University studying Maths and Logic."

"I know what Maths is," says the new bloke, "but what the fuck is logic?"

"Ah says the first bloke", pleased to have the opportunity to demonstrate his new found knowledge, "You've got a fish tank at home right?"

"No" says the new bloke.

"What are you, some kind of a fucking pervert?"

THE OLD SHOELACE SALESMAN

There's this little old man who sits on the pavement outside the head office of this huge multi-national corporation selling shoelaces – 20p a pair.

Every day at 5.30, the Chief Executive of the company leaves the building to get into his chauffeur-driven Rolls, but before he does, he always goes over to the little old man, puts 20p on his tray and never takes the laces.

This goes on for twenty years and neither of them ever speak a word - 20p on the tray, never takes the laces, into the Roller and off.

Then one day, the Chief Exec leaves the building, goes and puts his 20p on the tray (doesn't take the laces), and is just getting into the back of the Rolls when he hears this voice saying "Excuse me."

He looks around and the little old man is beckoning him over. He hesitates a bit, but eventually walks back over to him and bends down.

And the little old man looks up at him and says "They've gone up!"

ORAL SEX

A dark and dirty job, but someone's gotta do it!

Arthur and his mates were talking in the pub about Oral Sex. Arthur had never done that with his missus and said he didn't fancy it, it must taste horrible.
But Mike, Arthur's mate, said what he needed was a few extra drinks and just to go home, straight into the bedroom, dive under the Duvet, and go for it.
Don't ask; Don't hesitate, Don't take No for an answer!

Arthur weaved his way home from the pub late that night, well oiled and feeling that this was the night!

He crept up the stairs as quietly as he could, taking off his shoes and socks. Along the landing he undid his trousers and stepped out of them, and took his shirt off as he went into the bedroom, which was pitch black. He could hear the contented sound of quiet snoring.

At the end of the bed, he slipped his head under the duvet, found her legs and gently caressed them and kissed all the way up the inside of her thighs until he came to beaver country. Ignoring the images of Trawlers that his mind was conjuring up, he found his way through the half acre of brambles, and went to work with his tongue.

She moaned and heaved, and heaved and moaned some more and eventually with an almighty push upwards, he felt a gush of hot juices running down his chin. As she sagged back down, he slipped out the bottom of the bed and crept to the bathroom for a wash, feeling very satisfied with himself.

Suddenly, a familiar voice whispered from inside the bath "Do you mind sleeping in the spare room tonight darling, Mother's staying and I've let her have our bed!"

SELL UP - SELL UP - SELL UP!

A new lad started in the general store and was being trained by Derek, the most experienced and silver-tongued old salesman the company had.

"The thing to do lad, to get yer bonuses," said Derek, "is to sell the customers more than they came in to buy."
"How'd you do that" said the lad
You watch me with this customer he said.

"Good Morning Sir, How can I help you this fine sunny day?"
"Oh I'd like some grass seed please" said the man.
"Certainly Sir, we have rye grass, pampas grass, bowling green grass......."
"Oh I think rye grass will do fine" said the customer.
"Absolutely sir, makes a very fine lawn, which will be a pleasure to cut and admire and talking about cutting, how's the lawnmower these days, nice and sharp; been serviced for the new season has it"
"Well no it hasn't............." said the customer
"Did you know we do some wonderful deals on lawnmowers" continued Derek. "We have simple but lightweight hand mowers, the very latest electric mowers, petrol mowers, diesel mowers, sit-on and ride mowers, they'll all make your newly sown lawn look wonderful in a months time"
And sure enough, the customer bought a brand new lawnmower for £300.
"There, said Derek to the lad, "that was easy wasn't it.
Always remember, sell up, try to sell them more than they came in to buy – sell up – sell up – sell up!"
"Here comes another customer, you take this one, I'll be on your shoulder in case you need help."

The lad said "Good morning Madam, How can I help you"
"I'd like a packet of Tampax please," she said.
"Oh" said the lad, a bit flustered at this and still thinking "lawnmowers" and "sell-up."
"How about a nice lawnmower instead," he stammered.
"What do I want one of those for," she demanded.
The lad was getting increasingly agitated, and blurted out,
"Well it looks like your weekend's fucked, so you might as well cut the lawn!"

THAT FERRET SUCKS!

Man walked into his local and saw a ferret on the bar.
He said to the Barman "What on earth have you bought that thing in here for?

The barman said "That my friend, is a very very special ferret!"
"This ferret can give a blow job better than any woman in the world!"

"Oh what a load of crap" said the customer.

The Barman said "Go ahead, have one on the house."
So the man stuck the ferret down his kegs and WOW! What a blow job!

After Dinner CLASSIC!

He was stunned and instantly offered the barman £50 for the ferret.

"Not A Chance" said the barman, "it cost me £150."

"OK, £250" said the man. "Nope" the barman said adamantly.

"Look, my final offer – £500" said the man.

"Okay" said the barman, "that's a reasonable profit, it's yours."

The man took the ferret home and had another quickie just to prove it was no trick.
Incredibly, this was better than the first.

Whilst he was sitting at the kitchen table somewhat boggle-eyed and knackered, his wife came home.

"What the hell is that thing doing in my kitchen" she yelled.
He looked at her and said,
"Shut your mouth; teach it to cook, then fuck off."

The Naughty Pet Shop Parrot!

A Woman went into a Pet Shop and said "I'd like a Parrot" please.

"I've only got one left" said the owner.
"He's very pretty isn't he," said the lady.
"Yes, but I must warn you, his language is a little ripe. He used to live in a brothel until 4 days ago."

"Oh don't worry about that", she said, "he'll soon get used to his new home and the language will disappear if we don't encourage him."

So the lady took him home.
She set his cage up and as soon as she took the cover off, he said,
"Fuck me – a new brothel; great stuff!"
The Lady said "That'll do, you watch your language."
The Parrot said, "Fuck me – a new brothel; new madam."
Then the parrot went quiet.

Later, the ladies daughter came home and the Parrot squawked,
"Fuck me! – new brothel, new madam, new prostitutes."
And got told off again.

At dinner time that evening the father of the house came in and the Parrot suddenly squawked up again,
"Fuck me! – new brothel, new madam, new prostitutes
– same old customers. Hello George, how are you?"

What's Eating You?

Three Women were talking over a cup of tea one day, when the younger one said, "I've got something to confess"
We are so hard up that I've had to go out on the game.
I'm so upset and don't want to humiliate my family."

Her Mother gave her a cuddle and said "Well my dear, you're not the first to do that in this family. Both me and your Grandmother there, have been on the game in our time, so we understand how you feel."

"How much do you charge these days dear" said the mother to her daughter.
"Oh £50 if I can get it" she replied.

"That's Fantastic, My best charge was only £20."

"How much did you charge Granny when you did it?"

"Oh when I was on the game, it was War time, so things were very different then. I didn't make a charge, but I only did Blow Jobs."

"Why was that then Granny."

"Well dear, it was very tough in the War and especially in the Winter months with no coal, I used to do blow jobs for Free because you never knew where your next hot drink was coming from!"

Skittles Night

Jethro's cousin Shirley, was coming to stay for a few weeks, and one night she asked what they did about a bath, as she had not seen a bathroom in the house. Jethro's wife said, "we use a tin bath in front of the AGA in the kitchen."

Shirley asked when she could have one.
Jethro's wife said; "Best night is Thursday, when Jethro goes out to skittles for the evening."

The next Thursday, they set the bath up in front of the kitchen AGA and filled it up with hot water.
Cousin Shirley was a bit embarrassed about undressing but Jethro's wife told her that all ladies had the same bits and that she had seen it all loads of times and would take any notice. So Shirley got in the bath and had a good wash.

Later that night as they were in bed, Jethro's wife said, "Jethro, do you know, your cousin Shirley hasn't got no hairs on her fanny."
Jethro said " Hasn't she, she's 49, she ought to have one or two by now. I'd like to see that."
Jethro's wife said "Well why not come home a bit early next Thursday from skittles and I'll leave a gap in the kitchen window curtains so you can have a little peep through."

So next Thursday, Shirley's having a bath and Jethro's wife commented, "I couldn't help but notice Shirley, that you have no hairs around your fanny."
"Should I have?" said Shirley.
"Well you should have a few by now" said Jethro's wife.
"Have you got any then?" said Shirley.
"Well course I have," said Jethro's wife and promptly lifted up her skirt and pulled her drawers down to show her about half an acre of brambles.

Twenty minutes later, Jethro came in and his wife said, "Well did you see she's got no hairs on her fanny?"
"Yes I bloody did", he yelled, "but what did you have to go showing her yours for?"
"Well there's nothing wrong with that, you seen mine many a time anyway"
"Yes I know I have," he said, "but the bloody skittles team haven't!"

Two Lovely Black Eyes

Gerald was in the pub Sunday lunchtime when his close friend Derek burst in sporting a fresh black eye.

"Derek, you got a black eye you have, you got a black eye. How you get that?"

"Well" said Derek, "I was in church this morning and this woman was sat in front of me wearing a silky frock, and as it was quite hot in church today, when she got up from praying, the frock had got stuck between the cheeks of her "harse. "Well I thought that this didn't look too good, so I lean forward and pull it out for her, and she turn round and clocks me right in the eye."

After Dinner CLASSIC!

Gerald said " Derek, I told you before, it ain't none of your business, if she wants to take in washing, you leave her alone, it's none of your business."

The following week on the Sunday Lunchtime, Derek bursts into the pub sporting two black eyes.

Gerald says "Derek, what have you been doing today, you now got two black eyes, you have, how you get that?"

"Remember that woman last week" replied Derek, "well she was there sat in front of me again, and wearing that same silky frock as last week, and it was quite hot and sticky in church today, and sure enough, the dress got caught up between the cheeks of her "harse" again, just like last week."

"Well this chap near me, he thought that didn't look too good either and he lean forward and pull it out, but I knew from last week, that she don't like that, so I lean forward with my finger, and push it back in, and she clocked me in the other eye this time!"

More Quickies

Toilet Graffiti at Microsoft

Bill Gates downloads here

~~~~~~~~~~~~~~~~~~~~~

I went to see the Bank Inspector the other day and said,
"I'd like to open a joint account."

He said, " Who with?"

I said, "You, you stupid Bastard."

~~~~~~~~~~~~~~~~~~~~~

An Accountant arrived at the Pearly Gates and said "there must be some mistake, I'm not due up here yet, I'm only 41"!

Peter says, "Just a minute, I'll check our records again."

He looks at the accountant and says, "Sorry old chap, according to the time you've logged to your clients, you're 125!"

~~~~~~~~~~~~~~~~~~~~~

Just A Few More
Media Gaffes!

**"Julian Dicks is everywhere.
It's like they've got eleven Dicks on the field."**
(*Metro Radio*)

~~~~~~~~~~~~~~~~~

"....and later we will have action from the men's cockless pairs...."
(*Sue Barker*)

~~~~~~~~~~~~~~~~~

"There goes Juantorena down the back straight, opening his legs and showing his class."
(*David Coleman at The Montreal Olympics*)

A Headache again?

One evening a man emerged naked from the bathroom and was
climbing into bed when his wife moaned as usual,
"I have a headache"
"Well its your lucky night" he replied,
"I was just in the bathroom powdering my penis with Aspirins."

~~~~~~~~~~~~~~~~~~~~~~~~

Beware the Wooden Fence!

A Man was walking down the street past a mental institution,
which had a high wooden fence around it. He heard a number of
people chanting 19...19...19... and he became curious.
He found a knothole in the wooden fence big enough to see
through, bent over and peered in. Immediately, he was poked in the
eye by a finger and the chant changed to 20...20...20...!

BE FIRM!

One morning a man walked up to his wife and pinched her on the bottom and said " Dear, if you firmed this up a bit, you could get rid of your girdle." She bit her tongue but said nothing.

The next morning, her husband woke up and grabbed hold of a breast and said, "You know, if you firmed these up a bit, you could get rid of your bra."

With anger seething, she rolled over and grabbed hold of his tackle and said,

"You know, if you firmed this up a little more often, we could get rid of the Postman, Gardener, Milkman and your Brother."

~~~~~~~~~~~~~~~~~~~~~~~~~~~~

A man was standing waiting a long time for a bus, but was becoming increasingly fidgety, as he was getting desperate for a piss. Looking down at the wooden fence next to him he saw a knothole large enough to slip his JT through. Wriggling up to it, he slipped it in the hole and immediately something grabbed it the other side. He looked quickly over the fence to see 3 boys there.

The 1st one, about 9, said, "Give us a £1 or we'll cut yer cock off." The man said, "This is an enterprising business, how much money have you made today?" The boy said, "£18." The man looked at the next boy, about 7, and said "And how much money have you made?" "only £5, cos my hands are smaller." He looked at the smallest boy, about 4 and said "And have you made any money at all?"

"No," said the boy, "but I've got a bucket full of cocks!"

It All Happens in the Locker Room!

Three women were changing in the gym locker room, when a guy runs through, naked apart from a bag over his head. As he passes the first woman, she looks at his penis and says, "He's not my husband."

The second woman also says, "He's not my husband either," not recognising the unit.

The third woman says, "Wait a minute, he's not even a member of this club!"

The Last Rites

A wife is told by her doctor that she has only 12 hours to live.
So she and her husband decide to spend their last night together
wining and dining.
It's pretty late and they're having a wonderful time.

She says, "Darling, have another brandy."
He says, "No, I won't thank you."
She says, "Please have another brandy, we're enjoying ourselves."
He says, "No! Its all right for you, you haven't got to get up in the
morning."

Cock-a-doodle-doo!

There were three cockerels:
One was normal
One was dyslexic
And the third one was Gay.

Every morning the first one would get up and sing out
Cock-a-doodle-doo!

Then the second one would get up and sing
Dock-a-coodle-doo!

Finally the third would get up and sing
Any cock'll doo!

~~~~~~~~~~~~~~~~~~~~~~~~

Authentic Doctor Story

While acquainting himself with a new elderly patient, the doctor
asked, "How long have you been bedridden?" After a look of
complete confusion the old lady answered, "Why, not for about
twenty years, when my husband was alive."

~~~~~~~~~~~~~~~~~~~~~~~~

****

A lady walked into a pharmacy and spoke to the pharmacist. She asked:
"Do you have Viagra?"
"Yes," he answered.
She asked, "Does it work?"
"Yes," he answered.
"Can you get it over the counter?" she asked.
"I can if I take two," he answered.

****

A wife's place is by her husband's side

A woman's husband had been slipping in and out of a coma for several months, yet she had stayed by his bedside every single day.

One day, when he finally came to, he motioned for her to come nearer.
As she sat by him, he whispered, eyes full of tears,
"You know what? You have been with me all through the bad times...

When I got fired, you were there to support me.
When my business failed, you were there.
When I got shot, you were by my side.
When we lost the house, you stayed right here.
When my health started failing, you were still by my side...

You know what?"

"What dear?" She gently asked, smiling as her heart began to fill with warmth.

"I think you're bad luck ....

Why don't you fuck off!"

Even More Quickies

"Doctor, Doctor, I can't pronounce my F's, T's and H's."
"Well you can't say fairer than that then."

~~~~~~~~~~~~~~~~~~~~~~~~~~~

Little Johnny goes to school, and the teacher says, "Today we are going to learn multi-syllable words, children.
Does anybody have an example of a multi-syllable word?"

Little Johnny waves his hand, "Me, Miss Rogers, me, me!"
Miss Rogers, "All right, Johnny, what is your multi-syllable word?"
Little Johnny says, "Mas-tur-bate."
Miss Rogers smiles and says, "Wow, little Johnny, that's a mouthful."
Little Johnny says, 'No, Miss Rogers, you're getting mixed up with blow job."

~~~~~~~~~~~~~~~~~~~~~~~~~

Fuel For Thought

During the first fuel blockade in England, Sept 2000, a motorist went into a garage with no fuel and asked the attendant if he could fill up with Paraffin.
The attendant said, "Why on earth do you want to do that?"

The man said, "Well there's 2 F's in Paraffin, but there's no eff in Petrol!"

BR-HARE RABBIT

A man was driving along the highway, and saw a rabbit hopping across the middle of the road. He swerved to avoid hitting the rabbit, but unfortunately the rabbit jumped in front of the car and was hit. The driver, being a sensitive man as well as an animal lover, pulled over to the side of the road, and got out to see what had become of the rabbit.
Much to his dismay, the rabbit was dead.

The driver felt so awful, he began to cry. A woman driving down the highway saw the man crying on the side of the road and pulled over. She stepped out of her car and asked the man what was wrong.

"I feel terrible," he explained, "I accidentally hit this rabbit and killed it."

The woman told the man not to worry. She knew what to do. She went to her car trunk, and pulled out a spray can. She walked over to the limp, dead rabbit, and sprayed the contents of the can onto the rabbit.

Miraculously the rabbit came to life, jumped up, waved its paw at the two humans and hopped down the road. 50 yards away the rabbit stopped, turned around, waved and hopped down the road, another 50 yards, turned, waved and hopped another 50 yards.

The man was astonished. He couldn't figure out what substance could be in the woman's spray can!!

He ran over to the woman and asked, "What is in your spray can? What did you spray on that rabbit?"

The woman turned the can around so that the man could read the label. It said: "Hair spray. Restores life to dead hair. Adds permanent wave."

The Far-reaching Effect of Phillip Neville's Tackle!

The England footballer, Phillip Neville's mis-timed tackle that gave away a penalty and effectively knocked England out of Euro 2000 is allegedly directly attributable to a earthquake scare!

Tuesday night June 20th 2000, during England's Euro 2000 game against Romania, at precisely 9:28pm BST, scientists at the British Geological Survey recorded an earthquake measuring 4.7 on the Richter Scale.

The tremor which was detectable throughout the world, had it's epicentre in England and is thought to have been caused by 21 million people shouting the word w@nker simultaneously.

~~~~~~~~~~~~~~~~~~~~~~~~~~~~~~~~

One for the girls.....

Why do men snore when they lay on their backs?

Because their balls fall over their assholes and they vapour lock!

Another one for the girls

What do electric trains and breasts have in common?

They're intended for children, but it's the men who usually end up playing with them.

Two Burgers & A Hot Dog!

Trelawny was real peckish and pulled up at the Burger Van at the side of the road for a snack.

"Two burgers and a hot dog please," he called to the large greasy woman behind the counter.

He watched her take two frozen burgers from the fridge and put one under each armpit.
"What on earth are you doing?" he cried.

"I am defrosting your burgers," she said.

"Well if that's how you do it, you'd better forget the hot dog

SKODA Speed

A man in a Jaguar passed a Skoda that had broken down by the side of the road. Being a kindly driver, he stopped and fixed a tow-rope to it and began towing it to the nearest garage.
After 10 minutes of towing, a Porsche passed them at high speed. The Jaguar driver was not going to be outdone by a Porsche, so, forgetting that he had a Skoda in tow, slammed his foot down and Jaguar and Porsche indulged in a high-speed race down the road, the Skoda and its occupant trailing wildly about at the end of the rope frantically trying to attract their attention and failing.

A Police car saw them and gave chase.
The Police driver radioed back to Headquarters "Sarge, you'll never believe this, I've just seen a Porsche and a Jaguar neck and neck doing 150 mph – and a bloke in a Skoda flashing his lights, hooting his horn and trying to overtake them!"

BIG MAN; SMALL TOWN

Joe grew up in a small town, then moved away to attend college and law school. He decided to come back to the small town because he could be a big man in this small town. He really wanted to impress everyone. He opened his new law office, but business was very slow at first.

One day, he saw a man coming up the path. He decided to make a big impression on this new client when he arrived. As the man came to the door, Joe picked up the phone. He motioned the man in, all the while talking. "No. Absolutely not. You tell those clowns in New York that I won't settle this case for less than one million. Yes. The Appeals Court has agreed to hear that case next week. I'll be handling the primary argument and the other members of my team will provide support.

Tell the District Attorney that I'll meet with him next week to discuss the details."

This sort of thing went on for almost five minutes. All the while the man sat patiently as Joe rattled instructions. Finally, Joe put down the phone and turned to the man. "I'm sorry for the delay, but as you can see, I'm very busy. What can I do for you?" The man replied, "I'm from the phone company. I came to hook up your phone."

~~~~~~~~~~~~~~~~~~~~~~~~~~~~~~~

Top Tip

Don't buy expensive 'ribbed' condoms, just buy an ordinary one and slip a handful of frozen peas inside it before you put it on.

How Differently Men & Women
View the Same Event......

* HER STORY:

He didn't phone me all day in work and when I called him he
hardly spoke. He was in a really odd mood when I got to the pub,
I thought it might have been because I was a bit late but he didn't
say anything much about it.

The conversation was quite slow going so I thought we should go
off somewhere more intimate so we could talk more privately.
So we went to this restaurant and he's STILL acting a bit funny
and I'm trying to cheer him up and start to wonder whether it's me
or something else.

I ask him, and he says no. But you know I'm not really sure.

So anyway, in the cab back to his house, I say that I love him and
he just puts his arm around me. I don't know what the hell this
means because you know he doesn't say it back or anything.

We finally get back to his place and I'm wondering if he's going
to dump me! So I try to ask him about it but he just switches
on the TV.

Eventually, I just come out and say it. "Are you seeing someone
else?" He says No, but I'm not convinced.

Reluctantly, I say I'm going to go to sleep. After about 10 minutes,
he joins me and we have sex. However, he still seemed really
distracted, and afterwards he just rolls over and goes to sleep. He
doesn't say goodnight or anything. I just wanted to leave. I dunno,
I just don't know what he thinks anymore. I mean, do you think
he's met someone else???....

*HIS STORY:
Shit day at work. Tired. Got a shag though.

Facelift

A man decides to have a face-lift for his birthday. He spends $5,000 and feels really good about the result.
On his way home he pops into the newsagent and buys a paper. Before leaving he says to the newsagent "I hope you don't mind me asking, but how old do you think I am?"
"About 35" was the reply.
"I'm actually 47 years old" the man says, feeling really happy.

After that he goes into the Fish & Chip shop to celebrate. Before leaving, he asks the same question, to which the reply is "Oh, you look about 29" This makes him feel really good.
Whilst standing at the bus stop he asks an old woman the same question.

She replies, "I am 85 years old and my eyesight is going. But when I was young there was a sure way of telling a man's age. If I put my hand down your trousers and play with your balls for ten minutes I will be able to tell your exact age."

Being as there was nobody around the man thought what the hell and let her slip her hand down his trousers.

Ten minutes later the old lady says "You are 47 years old."
Stunned the man says, "That was brilliant. How did you do that?"
The old lady replies, "I was behind you in the Fish & Chip shop!"

More Revenge For Women

How does a man show that he is planning for the future?
He buys TWO cases of beer.

What is the difference between men and government bonds?
The bonds mature.

Why is it difficult to find men who are sensitive, caring and good looking?
They all already have boyfriends.

What do you call a woman who knows where her husband is every night?
A widow.

Why are married women heavier than single women?
Single women come home, see what's in the fridge and go to bed. Married women come home, see what's in the bed and go to the fridge.

How do you get a man to do sit ups?
Put the remote control between his toes.

What did God say after creating Adam?
I must be able to do better than that.

What did God say after creating Eve?
Practice makes perfect.

How are men and parking lots alike?
Good ones are always taken; free ones are mostly handicapped or extremely small.

What is the one thing that all men at singles bars have in common?
They are married.

Man says to God: "God, why did you make woman so beautiful?"

God says "So you would love her."

"But God," the man says, " why did you make her so dumb"?

God says "So she would love you."

I Am From Minsk!

Madame opened the brothel door to see an elderly Jewish Man. His clothes were all dishevelled and he looked needy.

"Can I help you?" the Madame asked.

"I want Natalie," the old man replied.

"Sir, Natalie is one of our most expensive ladies, perhaps someone else..."

"No, I want Natalie."

Just then Natalie appeared and announced to the old man that she charges $1,000 per hour. The old man never blinked and reached into his pocket, and handed her ten $100 bills. The two went up to a room for an hour, when after the man calmly left.

The next night he appeared again demanding Natalie. Natalie explained that no one had ever come back two nights in a row, and that there were no discounts ...it was still $1,000 for one hour. Again, the old man took out the money, the two went up to a room, and he calmly left an hour later.

When he showed up the third consecutive night, no one could believe it.

Again, he handed Natalie the money and up to the room they went. At the end of the hour, Natalie questioned the old man.

"No one has ever used my services three nights in a row. Where are you from?"

The old man replied, "I am from Minsk."

"Really," replied Natalie, "what a coincidence. I have a sister who lives there."

"I know," said the old man. "She gave me $3,000 to give to you."

<u>And finally the last of the Light Bulb changes...</u>

How many HAIRDRESSERS does it take to change a light-bulb?
Five. One to change the bulb and four to stand around admiringly and say "Fabulous, Gary!"

~~~~~~~~~~~~~~~~~~~~~

How many PUNK ROCKERS does it take to change a light-bulb?
Two. One to change the bulb and one to kick the chair out from under him.

~~~~~~~~~~~~~~~~~~~~~

How many FEMINISTS does it take to change a light-bulb?
Five. One to change the bulb, two to discuss the violation of the socket, and two to wish secretly that they *were* the socket.

~~~~~~~~~~~~~~~~~~~~~

How many ROCK AND ROLL SOUND ENGINEERS does it take to change a light-bulb?
"Did you say something?"

~~~~~~~~~~~~~~~~~~~~~

How many SPANIARDS does it take to change a light-bulb?
Juan.

~~~~~~~~~~~~~~~~~~~~~

What's the difference between a pregnant girl and a light bulb?
You can unscrew a light bulb!

Can You Do Better?

A collection of stories like these takes a long time to put together and there will always be people that know lots of better jokes than these and will never be able to publish them.

Well, now you can!!

The PPGS publishing team is already well into the next collection and if you would like to submit a joke for book 2, then we will publish it, give you a credit and send you a free copy of the next book.

Please send your joke or story, in writing to:
PPGS
PO Box 42
Princes Risborough
Bucks.
HP27
0XH

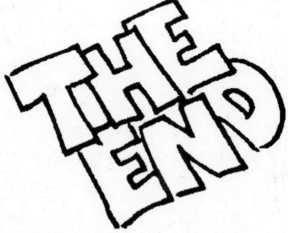